Child of Peace, Lord of Life

Reflections on the lectionary
from the First Sunday of Advent
to the Fifth Sunday in Lent, Year C

Herbert O'Driscoll

Anglican Book Centre
Toronto, Canada

1988
Anglican Book Centre
600 Jarvis Street
Toronto, Ontario
Canada M4Y 2J6

Copyright © 1988 Anglican Book Centre

All rights reserved. No part of this book may be reproduced, stored in a retrieval system, or transmitted, in any form or by any means, electronic, mechanical photocopying, recording, or otherwise, without the written permission of the Anglican Book Centre.

Typesetting by Jay Tee Graphics Ltd.

Canadian Cataloguing in Publication Data

O'Driscoll, Herbert, 1928-
  Child of peace, lord of life : reflections on the readings of the Common Lectionary

ISBN 0-919891-82-9 (Year C, v. 1).

1. Bible – Criticism, interpretation, etc.
2. Bible – Liturgical lessons, English.
I. Title.

BS511.2.037 1986   220.6   C86-094825-0

*for Rick and Cathy
whose gifts and companionship
made it possible to find time
to write*

Contents

Suggestions for the use of these reflections 7
First Sunday of Advent 9
Second Sunday of Advent 18
Third Sunday of Advent 26
Fourth Sunday of Advent 34
Christmas — at Midnight 42
First Sunday after Christmas 51
The Baptism of the Lord, Proper 1 62
Second Sunday after Epiphany, Proper 2 71
Third Sunday after Epiphany, Proper 3 80
Fourth Sunday after Epiphany, Proper 4 89
Fifth Sunday after Epiphany, Proper 5 98
Sixth Sunday after Epiphany, Proper 6 108
First Sunday in Lent 117
Second Sunday in Lent 125
Third Sunday in Lent 134
Fourth Sunday in Lent 143
Fifth Sunday in Lent 152

Acknowledgement

The two stanzas and two lines of Sir John Betjeman's "Christmas" are reprinted from *Collected Poems* by permission of John Murray (Publisher) Ltd.

Suggestions for the Use of These Reflections

My intention is that these pages be helpful to anyone who may have the responsibility of giving homilies in the contexts of worship or of leading Bible study based on the Sunday scriptures. They might also be helpful to anyone who wishes to prepare for worship by having some possible applications of scripture suggested for reflection.

At no time do I want to suggest that these reflections are *the* meaning of a particular passage. Most certainly there are particular meanings to every scripture, and it is the task of exegesis to seek those meanings. It is equally true, however, that scripture, like all great literature, is infinitely rich in its capacity to evoke an endless variety of responses in those who come to it. Two thousand years of Christian reflection and three thousand years of Jewish reflection are ample proof of this.

1 Each of these chapters looks at the Old Testament, the Epistle and the Gospel in that order, then the Psalm. I have chosen to do this because very often the Psalm is an expression of themes which may be spread through two or even three of the readings.

2 I think it important to note that each chapter is not structured as a homily. Each reading is taken as significant in itself. Naturally, I have always listened for echoes of one reading in the others, yet my primary goal has been to let each scripture speak with its own integrity. Because of this there will very often be material for homilizing within the treatment of any one reading.

3 Because the full scripture text is readily available to any reader, I have quite often not given the complete sequence of a verse. No such omission is an attempt to manipulate a convenient meaning from scripture.

4 It will be noted that in many cases I have given more space to the first reading. I have done this to encourage the developing recovery of the Old Testament as a source of homily.

5 It may be worth saying a word about the lectionary as having a weekly theme. This is not always immediately evident. Sometimes it simply does not do so. While the compilers of the lectionary have assumed the Gospel to be the primary reading, each of the three readings, because of its being part of an ongoing sequence in its own particular book of the Bible, will sometimes have its own "word" for the reader. Certainly, links are always possible, but they are not necessarily ready-made, waiting to be built into a neat three-part homily or meditation or Bible study! However, to the extent that it may be helpful to point out possible patterns and links, I have tried to express an overall theme for each set of readings.

6 These reflections have one purpose. They are not designed to be in themselves merely the material for someone else's preaching or meditation or Bible study. They will have been most richly of use to the extent that they act as a starting point and catalyst for the reader's own reflections.

First Sunday of Advent

Jeremiah 33.14–16
1 Thessalonians 3.9–13
Luke 21.25–36
Psalm 25.1–9

Theme All the readings are, in different ways, about the need to have a trusting relationship with God. The Jeremiah passage speaks of an implicit trust in the future, and this is remarkable because there was very little reason for such confidence at the time! Paul prays for the Thessalonica community that the bonds of loving trust among them, and in God, may grow. Luke tells of Our Lord's surprising advice for living at a time when everything seems to be in turmoil!

First Reading *Behold, the days are coming, says the Lord, when I will fulfil the promise I made*

The situation behind this statement of Jeremiah was about as ghastly as it could possibly be. A terrible threat of invasion loomed over the people. That threat was to become reality. The Babylonian armies were soon to arrive with all the terrible consequences of any armed invasion. If we know this, we begin to realize the significance of the passage. Time after time voices of the Old Testament express hope. We know that and we are familiar with it. But the magnificent quality of this hope lies in the fact that there is almost no logical or tangible evidence for it! That is its greatness. The peculiar gift of Judaism is to hope in the face of there being apparently no hope!

Does that apply to us today? It certainly applies to some of the great issues of our time, such as the nuclear threat and the population explosion and the environmental upheaval. Sometimes these things seem so vast that we fall helpless before them. Such is our feeling of helplessness that many people cannot even discuss the issues. Very often in church life we resent their being mentioned in either sermon or announcements. Our anger is the measure of our hopelessness about being able to affect the situation in any way. Hopelessness breeds a sense of helplessness and thus brings about the very things we dread!

> *I will fulfil the promise I made*

In the soul of Judaism there is always the conviction that, whatever the future may be, God is within that future. We very badly need that conviction in western Christianity. Our culture puts very great pressure on us to fall into the trap of thinking of God as the god of the past, the god of a long and fine tradition, but somehow not the god of the present. We are dangerously near a concept of God as mere memory! There is a feeling that present events have got away from God, are out of God's reach! We need very badly to recapture a natural sense of God as God, in no sense the prisoner of these human illusions we call past, present, and future.

> *I will cause a righteous Branch to spring forth. . . he shall execute justice and righteousness*

Always in the vision of the future the voices of the Bible see the elements of justice and righteousness. The biblical vision is not merely about the coming of nice comfortable things! The Bible does not sing of "blue birds over the white cliffs of Dover" or, if it does speak of peace and harmony, it never neglects to name the necessary factors to a genuine and worthwhile peace. In expressing the hope for a future better world the Bible always mingles the element of justice with righteousness. For the Bible a righteous society or a righteous person is not merely the description of a personal internal religious condition! The Bible probes what we mean by righteousness and asks if it includes justice! The Bible is a most uncomfortable book to read for this reason. The uncomfortable things we sometimes hear about justice are not always merely the ideas of trendy Christians who have exchanged the Holy Spirit for left-wing politics. These same ideas await us in the Bible and defy us to skirt around them or ignore them.

> *Judah will be saved and Jerusalem will dwell securely. And this is the name by which it will be called: 'The Lord is our righteousness'*

Jeremiah seems to be saying that their society will be secure only to the extent that it becomes a society of justice and integrity. It will do that only if people come to realize that the nature of God, the nature of ultimate reality, is this thing Jeremiah calls righteousness. The biblical concept is very rich, and it is well worth looking up the many uses and nuances of meaning given to the word. When the Bible speaks of a righteous society, it means a society which reflects the nature and the will of God. We know well that no such society is ever going to exist within history, at least not in a final state. But the whole point is that such a vision calls us and will call men and women to work and to pray and to sacrifice in every age and every culture. It is a dream which never dies. It is so powerful a dream that it has even spilled out beyond the spiritual into the would-be secularism of classical Marxism. (We can say "would-be" because the very possession of the vision of a transformed society is proof that the official godlessness of Marxism is itself an illusion.)

> *Fulfil the promise [v 14]. . . . a righteous Branch [v 15]*

For the Christian reading this passage all such images are, of course, pointers to the expected one who comes toward us in this Advent season. In Our Lord Jesus Christ the Christian sees the embodiment of all ultimate values, and among them that justice and righteousness of which Jeremiah speaks.

Second Reading *For what thanksgiving can we render to God for you, for all the joy which we feel for your sake before our God*

Paul had an extraordinary gift for affirming people. (It was all the more a gift because he could affirm immediately after being very stern. The mixture is not present here in this letter but the ability to affirm certainly is.) Paul is communicating very clearly that for him it is a joy and privilege to have got to know the members of the Thessalonica community. This is a gift that both clergy and laity need in today's Christian community. Clergy, without ever expressing it in words, signal how they feel about their people, and the congregation develops a perception about a priest's feelings and attitude. It is essential that he or she communicate the kind of affirmation Paul is giving here in this passage. The message must be that he or she cares, that he or she finds it good to be among these people. If this is not heard or perceived, the possibilities for ministry are limited.

But the same is true of each member of the congregation. A congregation is a kind of being in itself, almost as if there is a reality beyond each of the people who make it up. The entire congregation, the gathering as a whole, is immensely strengthened if the members feel good about being part of it. Consequently, it is important that people pray for this strange, unwieldly, scattered, and infinitely varied thing we call our parish. The parish is a life form in its own right. Just as Thessalonica thrives on Paul's thanksgiving and joy for its community, so our local parish needs to feel that people are thankful they are part of it and are enjoying their participation in its life. (I realize that all this sounds rather like "Have you hugged your parish today?" yet here lies a very valuable truth for the church's life.)

Supply what is lacking in your faith

All parishes are incomplete and partial, all can be improved. The church building may have been finished for a century. The stewardship campaign can be eminently successful, the sermons brilliant, the pews full. But Our Lord Jesus Christ is still calling that community further than it has gone. Christ still asks for greater quality of spiritual life. Our Lord may desperately be trying to get the parish to realize that some aspects of its very successful life need to be evaluated and its energies rechannelled into areas which have been neglected. Paul himself in the following prayer mentions one thing that is paramount for a congregation's life.

May the Lord make you increase and abound in love to one another

That is Paul's challenge to today's parish. It needs to be more than an institution, more than an organization, more than a smoothly oiled machine. It needs to be a community where people feel some sense of acceptance and caring.

To one another and to all men

Paul's second demand on a congregation. Not only is it to offer caring and sensitivity among its own ranks, but also it must reach out beyond itself — something that may be more difficult to do.

So that he may establish your hearts unblamable in holiness

It is interesting to realize that Paul regards the two above qualities in a congregation's life as the measure of its "holiness." In both cases holiness is seen by Paul, at least in this context, as essentially a social thing, something that lives and thrives in the relationships within and beyond the life of a congregation.

Third Reading *There will be signs*

A most significant passage for the present time. This theme is never far from the modern mind; howsoever that mind may give it expression. We often hear it in the kind of preaching which uses the rhetoric of threat and judgement. But also we hear it creeping into contemporary thought and conversation. We are very attuned to this, of course because of the threats we have ourselves created, the nuclear threat being the most obvious but by no means the only one.

Our Lord was not saying anything new here. This kind of statement would have been familiar to him. He lived at a time when apocalyptic thinking was prevelant. Such thinking would have been equally familiar to those listening to him. Actually, when we take a look at the images of the passage, we begin to realize how telling they can be for our own time.

Signs in sun and moon and stars

There are indeed "signs" for us in the heavens. The word *sign* is related to the word *significant*. Space has become immensely significant for us. We have gone out there for the first time since our creation. That is bound to change us. We are trying to decide whether we can make a potential battleground of outer space! The future depends on such decisions. Space has become a moral and spiritual arena for us. It is full of signs.

Upon the earth distress of nations in perplexity

Consider the great difficulties facing every human institution at the present time. All political systems are under stress, their institutions and their methods striving desperately to serve the changing needs of humanity. All economic systems are under great strain. The old doctrines are barely able to explain or sustain viable societies, where there can be an acceptable distribution of wealth and the satisfactory employment of a new generation.

In perplexity at the roaring of the sea and the waves

Consider how challenged we are ecologically. We are particularly concerned about the lakes and seas and oceans of the world. Therein lies our very life. If we were to poison them we would die. "The sea and the waves" have indeed become for us a sign of great concern.

> *Men fainting with fear and foreboding of what is coming on the world*

The contemporary experience of that is the diffuse and universal anxiety of our time. Any doctor or psychiatrist or priest or social worker, anyone who has anything to do with the human condition, will tell us that life today is infiltrated by a general and constant and largely unfocused anxiety. It plays havoc with us mentally, physically, and spiritually if we do not in some sense share it. To deal with it we very much need a caring community. We also will find that the very act of worshipping, of directing our hearts and minds beyond ourselves to that which is beyond and above and around us, can be healing in the deepest and most transforming way.

> *The powers of the heavens will be shaken*

For us now, everything is being shaken. History, human affairs and experience, human assumptions and traditions. All require reassessment, rethinking. Faith itself is being shaken.

> *Look up and raise your heads, because your redemption is drawing near*

Jesus' remark here must have surprised them. It is positive, hopeful, an invitation to participation and confidence. What can that mean for us? It can influence our attitude to present events. We can see them as prelude to an ending, a defeat, a wiping out of the kind of world we know, or we can see them as the prelude to a new beginning. The process in between is painful and often frightening and undeniably dangerous. But a very valid Christian hope is that God is forming the next chapter of human history. To have such a hope is not in any way trivializing or lessening the power of this scripture. Strangely some people feel that one is slightly un-Christian not to regard the possibility of the end of the world with lip-smacking relish! Without in the least denying that there will in God's time come an end to the created order, our Christian duty is to do what Jesus spends the rest of this passage telling us to do, to live creatively and responsibly in the present age, responding to God's call to be his people.

Psalm

A song that begins with trust, that trust called for in the first and third reading. There is a very reasonable human wish to understand the ways of God (v 3). We cannot always understand those ways and we should admit it readily. The psalmist is really asking God that the capacity to trust may remain whatever happens. That, of course, is our prayer about our own lives.

Second Sunday of Advent

Malachi 3.1–4
Philippians 1.3–11
Luke 3.1–6
Psalm 126

Theme All the scriptures speak of a messenger and a message. We are warned that God's messenger and God's message can break into human affairs without warning (Malachi). Paul, acting as messenger to the community in Philippi, brings a message of immense affirmation and encouragement (Philippians). Among many figures of power who see themselves as conveying commands of that power, only one bears the message which speaks of a new stance toward life (Luke).

First Reading *I send my messenger to prepare the way before me*

There is a long history in Judaism of looking for God's messenger. Especially during this season of the year, this passage prompts us to reflect on Our Lord as God's messenger. We might use this scripture to remind ourselves that God, eternally creating and forming history, gives us messages and messengers in every age. Certainly, for a Christian Our Lord is the supreme messenger, his words our supreme message, his birth, life, death, and resurrection the supreme truth about human life. Still we must ask how this Christian faith, with its insights about the human condition, can sensitize us to all the other ways in which God is involved in the total process of human experience and human events.

Another salutary message of this scripture is that, to some extent, each of us is called by baptism to be a messenger preparing the way of the Lord. Sometimes what we do and say, who we are essentially, can open the way for God to work in someone else's life.

> *The Lord whom you seek will suddenly come to his temple*

That is very true on a personal level. We seek God in many ways. Most of the time, in busy and sometimes frantic lives, the presence of God is distant and even unreal. Suddenly, for some reason, God will impinge upon us. It may be a moment of fear, of beauty, of worship, of prayer, of meditation. The same is true in the affairs of our time. A dangerous international confrontation, a breakthrough in the world of the sciences, an ethical dilemma in our treatment of human life — all such things can bring us face to face with a mystery above and beyond ourselves or our powers.

> *The messenger of the covenant in whom you delight*

Here is a suggestion for the kind of message we should be seeking from God. If I am committed to the belief that there does indeed exist a covenanted relationship with humanity and God, then I am also committed to searching for signs of the continuing of that covenant in the affairs of my own time. The covenant of the Bible is no good to us merely as a memory. If there is a breakthrough, however partial, in nuclear arms, I can look upon that as a glimpse, however faint or fragile, of the eternal covenant. If I see that an international body has agreed to lessen our chemical pressure on the all-important ozone layer around the planet, that too is a reflection of the eternal covenant between humanity and God and the created order. To hold the conviction that contemporary events occur within the context of a covenant eternally offered to humanity, whether or not we always play our part in that covenant, is to transform one's view of human events. One possesses a receptacle of meaning in which to place the contradictions and complexities of those events, not to mention their frequent tragedies.

> *He is like a refiner's fire and like fuller's soap. . . . who can stand when he appears*

Always there is a warning about searching for a message from God, or for the presence of God in our lives. Sometimes we may not like what we find! Sometimes what is given may not be what we wish. The journey of faith and covenant is sometimes costly.

Second Reading   *I thank my God in all my remembrance of you*

One of the truly happy letters of Paul's correspondence, Philippians gives us a glimpse of Christians achieving that very elusive quality — community. The frequency with which Paul appeals in his letters for a real quality of community is the measure of how difficult it is to achieve. If we fully realize the difficulty of community building in those early years of Christianity, we will no longer feel that our difficulties arise from some peculiar problems of today's world. Certainly there are reasons why contemporary community building is difficult, but it was never easy! The New Testament church is ample proof of that.

> *Making my prayer with joy, thankful for your partnership in the gospel*

Notice how affirming Paul is towards the community. This may seem so very obvious, but it is frequently missing from the way we relate and communicate with others. It is extraordinary how frequently we neglect affirmation of others. We often take it perfectly for granted that someone knows he or she is appreciated, their contribution valued, their company liked. Church life, far from being the exception, can be the place where there is a very high level of taking people for granted.

> *I am sure that he who began a good work in you will bring it to completion*

The second quality Paul communicates is optimism. It is invaluable in any project. Can it sometimes be unreal and unjustified? Of course it can, but that does not invalidate this most powerful, intangible resource! Sometimes one detects a kind of mindset among contemporary Christians, certainly among mainline Christians, that the best we can hope for is dogged survival! Such a stance is not conducive to the formation of living, active community.

> *I told you in my heart, for you are all partakers with me of grace*

We cannot emphasize too often that a Christian community is more than the sum of its parts. What you see is not what you get! You get more! That "more" is grace, the Holy Spirit, the presence of the living and loving God bringing life and love into human hearts and human plans and human projects!

> *Grace, both in my imprisonment and in the defence and confirmation of the gospel*

These may very well be challenging days for Christian faith. We may often feel in the prison of a largely antagonistic culture, in the prison of a marginalized church life, in the prison of our own frustration. There are many forms of that image of prison which Paul refers to. The essential thing is to realize that grace comes no less in our prisons than at any other time.

> *My prayer that your love may abound more and more, with knowledge and all discernment*

Notice how love is defined. It is not mere sentimentality. It is an aware loving. It is a love that remains, even after we have had to work together and have got to know one another's gifts and shortcomings. We know each other and we have had to develop discernment about each other, yet still we love. That is reality, not sentimentality.

> *So that you may approve what is excellent*

The gift Paul prays for here is that the community may be able to tell what is worthwhile for its life and what is not. We need that today. We need to determine the quality of many programs offered. We need the ability to evaluate a person's spiritual experience. Is it healthy or neurotic? Furthermore, when we do find something worthwhile, we need to get beyond it with everything we have got. Such statements may sound obvious and unsophisticated, but they express the essential ingredient missing from so much contemporary mainline Christian life, yet very much present in contemporary evangelical and fundamentalist Christian life — enthusiasm! commitment! confidence in God!

Third Reading   *In the fifteenth year of the reign of Tiberius Caesar*

Whether or not Luke consciously put this as the opening statement of this scene of his book, the single sentence is full of dramatic irony. As the great lens of Luke's vision shows us Rome in the person of Caesar, we realize two things. Rome is mighty. Rome is the context of all life in that ancient world. All men and women bow to Rome. A word from Rome and millions of people are uprooted to suit the whim of the emperor who wishes to make a census. This tiny country in which Luke sets us now is itself a pitiable province of Rome. Yet, irony of ironies, the Galilean of whom John speaks in this passage will humble Rome. Long after Rome dies this as yet unseen Galilean will be known in every country in the world, in empires which will dwarf anything Rome can imagine.

Pontius Pilate being governor of Judea

Again Luke is the consummate dramatist. A name, a face, a voice flash across our vision for a moment and then are gone, but we will meet this face again. The face and the name are linked by their title to power, yet this man will be shown to be pitiably weak.

Herod, tetrarch of Galilee. . . Philip, tetrarch of Ituraea. . . Lysanias, tetrarch of Abilene

Every one of them needs his title to give him substance. All are personally undistinguished, politically insecure. All are essentially compromised by their efforts to obtain their present status. All are puppets of Rome and viewed with contempt by the Roman administration.

The high priesthood of Annas and Caiaphas

Again we see clever compromised men whose energies are wholly devoted to political gamesmanship and to personal and national survival.

The word of the Lord came to John . . . in the wilderness

Deftly Luke draws his implicit contrasts. With John walks the companionship of God. The others by implication walk their pragmatic, self-serving ways without that presence, not because the presence of God is unavailable to them but because they have long forsaken it. Perhaps if asked about such embarrassing things they would say, as their twentieth-century descendants would say, that they were too busy living in the real world to bother about such optional things. From rulers in high places Luke turns to a prophet in the wilderness. That is where the word of God comes, not in the brittle sophistication of the tetrarch's court, or in the nervous authority of Pilate's residence, or even in the exalted palaces of Rome. God is found in the least expected place. It is very important for us to hear what Luke says in that single word *wilderness*, if only because contemporary life is lived in a wilderness of change and fear and threat and insecurity.

Preaching a baptism of repentance

Again a contrast. All the political figures that Luke names are engaged in preserving the status quo. Only John is the bearer of a vision of change. Only John sees that everything must turn around as a new age begins. That is exactly what he means by the cry to repentance. Both John and the others are with us in today's world and church. There are those who see no reason to change, usually for exactly the same reasons that motivated Luke's power sharers. The status quo is satisfactory from their point of view. They have done reasonably well from it. They do not see the wilderness because they take care never to go there. But in the wilderness is springing up the vision of a new reality, a new turning point of history. To what extent is this true in the wilderness of contemporary history? Where is the wilderness in our present time? Who are the voices which speak of the necessity to "turn around" in attitude, in lifestyle, in our vision of justice, in our quest for peace. What turning, or repenting, must be done?

Psalm

For the poet and for a whole people there has been a reversal of fortune. Where there was sorrow there is joy, for tears there is laughter, for death life. Have there been such times in our own lives? How did we feel? Did we celebrate in terms of just being lucky, or did we ascribe our turning point to God? Did we give thanks?

Third Sunday of Advent

Zephaniah 3.14–20
Philippians 4.4–9
Luke 3.7–18
Canticle 3, Song of
  Thanksgiving
  (BAS p.76)

Theme All three passages are a shout of confidence, trust, and commitment towards God. The prophet is determined to get across to his people that God is within the events of their history (Zephaniah). Paul is insisting that the richest resource men or women have for living life with joy and meaning is trust in Jesus Christ as the presence of God in their lives (Philippians). Even John the Baptist's seemingly grim statements are rooted in the reality of the God who challenges our humanity to measure up to God's vision of human society (Luke).

First Reading *Sing aloud . . . shout, O Israel! . . . The Lord has taken away the judgements against you*

All through this passage the same message is repeated. It is something so worthwhile for Israel that he repeats it as a refrain in different images. To sum this whole passage up in one phrase — Zephaniah is shouting out the joyous fact that God is for them! God is among them! God has not withdrawn! They are not naked before history. As I write these very words, I find myself doing exactly what Zephaniah did. Like him I want to say something so important and so exciting that I can't leave it alone! Like him I want to use different words to say it again and again. Why is this theme so important?

The King of Israel is in your midst

It is a sad fact that for millions of people today this is either a meaningless statement or one that they would like to believe but cannot. Millions, not all outside the church, feel that God is not in the midst of the contemporary world because it has outpaced the poor old gentleman! In his best-selling Canadian book, *Not Wanted on the Voyage*, Timothy Findley draws this caricature of God — a stumbling, slightly grumpy old man no longer in charge of anything but given some respect on the basis of past performance. It is not at all a bad portrait of the god that dwells in the mind of much of western civilization. The king of Israel is not in our midst. A pale shadow is a memory, a fond memory, perhaps, but still a memory. We very badly need to recapture a sense of the eternal God being as much the God of today as of all our yesterdays. A God who is merely a God of yesterday cannot be a God of earth's tomorrows. And there is every indication that without God in our tomorrow we will be very lonely and very vulnerable. That is why Zephaniah's cry is important.

The Lord has taken away the judgements against you

There is much guilt in the western soul. Modern humanity doesn't seem to like itself. This shows in our arts. We have realized that we have a very dark side. The Bible would say that we have become aware of our sinfulness. But the Bible also says that we have another side, that the light of God within our humanity is unquenchable, that it flickers in every one of us and blazes out of some great souls. The whole tone of our new liturgies draws us away from guilt to the celebration of our gifts, from what we have been to what in Christ we can be. The repeated cry of the new liturgies is Zephaniah's shout, that the Lord has taken away judgement and is ready to risk again calling us to a covenant, even though our track record of covenant keeping is abysmal!

> *Do not fear, O Zion; let not your hands grow weak*

So often Christian thinking posits a relationship with God in terms of our weaknesses. We most certainly do need redemption. We need forgiveness. We need grace. We need empowering. These needs cannot for a moment be denied. But some Christians forget that God is also a God who wishes us to offer our strengths and our gifts, our creative faculties, not in some way to challenge God, but in full and thankful realization that the source of our strengths and gifts and creative powers is God.

> *I will save the lame and gather the outcast*

Here it is again, something we always hear in the Bible when a renewed and transformed society is envisioned. There will be a place for the weak! They will not be marginalized. They will not be regarded as an embarrassing social phenomenon. The response of the society towards the weak and the poor and the wounded will itself be one of the foremost measures of the quality of the society.

Second Reading   *Rejoice in the Lord always*

I don't think for a moment that Paul meant that Christians must forever be happy. Human nature cannot possibly be eternally effervescent and euphoric. I think Paul is saying that if we believe in Jesus Christ as alive and near and real in our lives, then we can possess a sense of quiet joy about our lives. Our joy is that we possess a Lord, a focus, a resource, a "north pole" for the otherwise wandering compass of our own selves.

Let all men know your forbearance

I think a good modern word for forbearance might be *resilience*. There is a sense in which possessing a deep Christian faith can give one staying power in life, in spite of disappointments and, for some, even in the face of immense tragedy. We have all met people for whom, even in the most appalling situations, the Lord is at hand.

Have no anxiety about anything

The statement echoes Our Lord's "be not anxious." It's an enormous demand, and we need to be very realistic in our preaching about it. We should resolve never to say things to others which we are not ready to believe ourselves! I think it is possible to see this statement as an ultimate standard to be aimed at, with the certainty that only the rarest of great souls can enter that state. It calls us to a living of our lives in trust. The total absence of trust can be devastating in life. The scripture also implies that a constant all-pervading anxiety (all too common today) is simply not a reflection of mature Christian faith. There is almost always some aspect of daily life about which we can legitimately feel anxiety, if only for the fact that it would be inhuman not to. It is diffused and generalized anxiety we must watch carefully, the kind that we cannot define when we are asked to.

> *In everything by prayer and supplication with thanksgiving let your requests be made known to God*

There is much in these few phrases. "In everything." We have tended to cordon off the areas of life which we consider to be legitimate for prayer. Would we naturally pray about our business affairs, other than when we are desperate and frightened? Even personal areas are often foreign to prayer. Would we naturally pray about our sexuality, asking for its richness and joy in abundance with those whom we love? "Supplication with thanksgiving," an interesting linkage. Even when we are asking God for something, we need to retain a sense of gratitude for what we have already received.

> *And the peace of God, which passes all understanding, will keep your hearts and minds in Christ Jesus*

Here is one of those lyrical moments of scripture which we should be wary of trying to explain too literally. Its power lies in itself, a power attested to by its universal use in Christian liturgy as a blessing, and by its being set to music many times. The very sound of the words is itself healing and calming. For Christians this statement could well be what is called in other traditions a mantra, something said again and again while being reflected upon as one draws on its power and peace and beauty.

> *Finally . . . think about these things*

Paul is being very "Greek" at this moment. What he is saying is universally true. What we think about forms us; therefore we need to be intentional about our thinking. Thinking forms attitude, attitudes form moods, moods can issue in actions. We need to have access to sources of beauty, truth, purity, loveliness, and honour. These things form us, exactly as their opposites also form us.

Third Reading   *Bear fruits that befit repentance, and do not begin to say to yourselves, 'We have Abraham as our father'*

John is challenging a rather complacent society to take another look at itself. His words can be applied to any society in any age. What is not being seen? What need is being missed? If we think our society rather satisfactory in its institutions and its government, have we ever asked for whom it is satisfactory? Who is left out of the social contract? Can anything constructive be done about that?

What then shall we do?

This is an eternal question, asked in every age and in every society. Three classes of people ask the question of John. Notice what he does not say. He does not advise anyone to leave the world they are in, however morally ambiguous that world may be. John's first answer considers the need of society, and his appeal is for generosity on an individual basis. That would naturally be the way of his time. For us, such sharing has been taken over largely by the social institutions we have formed for the purpose. Yet, even though Christians may play their part in giving to institutions which respond to social need, perhaps we could also remain in touch with individuals and particular needs in order to help in a direct and personal way.

Collect no more than is appointed you. . . . Rob no one by violence or by false accusation

It may seem a statement of the obvious, but John is saying to these people and to us that, for the world to become a better place, each of us must conduct our affairs with integrity and compassion. This of itself will not eradicate the pain and injustice of society, yet it is a basic level of social responsibility we often forget, and a simple and effective starting point.

He who is mightier than I is coming

For John this event was imminent. Very soon Jesus was to come into public view, beginning a ministry in continuity with John's but also very different. For us the event can be very powerful in quite another way. Christians await the one who comes to judge. Christ as the Lord of history has given us a vision of a society where justice and peace and truth reign. Such are the images we encounter in Jesus' parables of the kingdom and in John's description of the Holy City. These images always judge and criticise even the best we can achieve in human society. They always draw us further, to greater commitment and achievement and social transformation. In the face of ultimate justice and peace and integrity in society, we feel "not worthy." These same images searingly show us the partial vision which is the best we can achieve ("wheat and chaff").

He preached good news to the people

This is an interesting summing up of all that John has said. Most has sounded grim and judgemental and critical. Yet to be told that more can be done, and that human affairs can be affected by a clear and uncompromising vision of something better, is essentially good news. It calls us to greater effort and inspires us to constantly renew our social vision.

Psalm
(Canticle 3)

The canticle primarily echoes the shout of the Zephaniah passage. We can reflect on the amazing ability of Israel to sing this song again and again in their history, even in the most appalling and dispiriting circumstances. Think of the places this song has been sung — in ancient Babylon, in Moorish Spain, in the Warsaw Ghetto, in Buchenwald. It makes one ask if the very singing of the song of trust makes further trust possible, and thereby gives a people, or indeed an individual, greater resilience in the face of circumstances.

Fourth Sunday of Advent

Micah 5.2–4
Hebrews 10.5–10
Luke 1.39–55
Psalm 80.1–7

Theme All the scriptures speak of the unexpectedness of God's actions. The prophet seems to suggest the most unlikely of places when he points to Bethlehem as the source of the future (Micah). The unknown writer declares the apparently impossible truth that God will provide in Our Lord the means of crossing the gulf between our humanity and the throne of God (Hebrews). Mary, overcome by the unexpectedness of the annunciation, comes to realize the paradoxical way God acts to confound the standards and methods of human judgement and assessment (Luke).

First Reading *But you, O Bethlehem. . . little among the clans of Judah*

Of the great themes which the Bible sings again and again, one is the theme of the unexpected action of God. God's actions continually, almost tantalizingly, remind humanity that, putting it very mildly, the divine mind is not merely the human mind writ large! If some great thing is to happen, human instinct will search for it in some great place. The event and the place must somehow have size and significance in common. Is that why almost all visiting spaceships in science fiction seem to land on the White House lawn? But I am quite sure that we can find science fiction stories in which the great event happens where there is almost nobody to take notice, at least nobody of seeming significance. To write such a story would be to understand and echo the great biblical truth about God's ways. God tends not to come to vast places of some particular political persuasion. God comes to the ordinary place and the ordinary person. In other words, God comes to us in our own lives! We are the small, ordinary Bethlehem which all undeservedly is given the gift, and of course, is also given the great responsibility.

> *Whose origin is from of old, from ancient days*

Let's go another way with this scripture. Let's go inward. Suppose I am myself the "Bethlehem" to whom God comes, as each of us can be. The Bible says to me that God brings forth a ruler from this ordinary, rather limited, Bethlehem which I am. In other words, God can bring out of me that which is more than my present ordinariness. This different "me" is not so much a new me but one which has always been hidden within me "from of old, from ancient days," only it has remained dormant until called out by God's grace.

> *Therefore he shall give them up until the time when she who is in travail has brought forth*

Can we continue with our above interpretation of this passage? Micah is saying that, until this person comes, Israel will feel lost, given up. As God works with us, trying to draw from us that which lies dormant within us, trying to get us to respond to his grace which is for our growth and renewing, we too may feel lost and given up, confused, feeling neither one thing nor the other.

> *And he shall stand and feed his flock in the strength of the Lord*

Still keeping with our personal and inward use of the scripture, are we being told something very important about our lives? When God brings out that larger and more whole person hidden within us, that part of us which awaits God's grace and God's call, then we shall be able to stand much more securely. We will also become a resource for others rather than being engaged so much in our own growth struggle that we are incapable of "feeding" others.

(Perhaps it is important to say that such an interpretation of the passage need in no way diminish its significance for Christians as an anticipating image of the coming of Our Lord.)

Second Reading   *When Christ came into the world*

In this letter the writer wishes to emphasize that the coming of Jesus Christ into the world has changed certain important things for ever, things which affect the relationship between our humanity and God. We are now about to be told one of those essential changes which Christ's coming brings about.

> *Sacrifices and offerings thou hast not desired*

For thousands of years, the writer suggests, there was a way in which humanity tried to stretch across the vast gulf it felt between itself and God. Humanity offered sacrifices from its own possessions, the poor offering small sacrifices, the rich very great ones. The sacrifice might also be graded by either the urgency of one's request of God or the guilt one felt before God. From time to time the prophets questioned this system, not because they thought it wrong but because they realized that it could become false. Unless an interior spirituality supported the exterior act, they felt sacrificing to be meaningless. They intuited quite correctly what was essential as humanity reached towards God — the offering of the self, whether in thanksgiving or remorse or self-dedication. All of this is not a discussion of a long-ago custom. The very same is true today. Often in our relationships we rely on exterior things as substitutes when we are not ready to respond to demands made on us. We will offer sacrifices to a spouse or to our child in the shape of money and gifts when, in fact, our loved one wishes desperately for part of our essential being, our time, our conversation, our listening, our understanding, our attention!

A body hast thou prepared for me

Now, the writer suggests, this is exactly what God has done. God has provided someone, Our Lord Jesus Christ, to give of his deepest self to the humanity/God relationship. He won't offer external sacrifices, but he will actually offer the totality of himself. Just as sacrifices involve slain birds and animals, he too will give his very body. The difference, the absolutely essential difference, is that this particular sacrifice is not outside our humanity but is actually the very essence of it. If I want to, I can reap the rewards of that sacrifice of Our Lord. If I am prepared to identify with him, to regard him as Lord of my life, then he has offered to God part of my personal humanity. The bridge of my Lord's humanity allows me to cross the gulf between God and me, in fact it eradicates the gulf! Thanks be to God. That is the essential message of this great passage of scripture.

I have come to do thy will

Repeatedly that word *will* is mentioned in this passage. The deepest element of sacrifice you and I can offer to God is to search out, and to try to do, God's will rather than merely our own will. That is true sacrifice, because it offers to God the self and the self's will. My self-will can be utterly a tyrant if I allow it. My vocation is to place it under the discipline and guidance of the will of God, to the extent that my partial and sinful humanity can discern that will.

Third Reading *Mary arose and went with haste*

Notice the very human touch of the words "with haste." In these few verses there is a great deal of humanity revealed. She had probably told Joseph of her experience and had seen the confusion of responses in his expression. The myths of the Graeco-Roman world around them were full of such births. It was quite another thing when one had to respond to it in actuality. Also, Mary would not have had any illusions about what lay ahead for them both. The village they lived in was an earthy and brutally harsh community. It would voice its varied and vivid opinions about her condition in the months ahead. Perhaps from such thoughts she came to the conclusion that the only place she might expect help and real understanding would be from someone else in the same condition, another woman who was herself pregnant. She knew of such a woman.

She entered the house of Zechariah and greeted Elizabeth

Is there a slight suggestion that Zechariah is passed by in the urgency of Mary to be close to Elizabeth. The moment of their meeting is extremely physical and ecstatic. Zechariah becomes very much the bystander and spectator. For this moment both Joseph and Zechariah become bystanders. Here we have an image of how many men feel today, aware that extraordinary elements of new life are forming in contemporary woman, but feeling strangely outside much of the process, relegated to the place of a mystified and sometimes even alarmed spectator?

Another nuance of this moment is that, as Mary takes her journey, she is a very contemporary figure. She goes a long way out of her own community to find acceptance and understanding. Our need and our search for community is a very complex thing. It need not always be found among those nearest us. It may be that in our North American society of mobility and transcience, our real community is with others who may now be far away. We seldom see them, but from some former intimacy or shared experience they have become and remain for us kindred spirits. Even though we may not have met for some years they understand us and we them. We feel that we can always turn to them, that they will always understand, that they and we can always take up from where we left off. It would seem that, for Mary, her cousin Elizabeth was such a person.

Blessed are you among women, and
blessed is the fruit of your womb

There is nothing but immediate affirmation from Elizabeth. There is no tentative acceptance, no careful questioning, no helpful sympathizing. With Elizabeth there is no doubt. This is gloriously right. This is reason to celebrate. Elizabeth gives Mary the one gift she wishes above all else, support and affirmation. For us all, such moments occur, and it is important to know them.

Someone may come to us in an agony of doubt about some event. We can see that whatever has happened there is no way back. All that is positive must now be emphasized. When we realize this, we should move towards the positive as strongly and as affirmingly as possible. Problems can be dealt with later. For now we must help the other person to grasp a sense of the possibilities of the situation. That is a real gift we can offer.

My soul magnifies the Lord

The effect of Elizabeth's support and love is immediate for Mary. She is given permission to sing! Her spirit can rejoice. She has been enabled to see a situation, albeit a difficult and even frightening one, as an opportunity for vocation and fulfilment. Sometimes to help someone do that is the greatest gift we can give. This is Elizabeth's gift.

He has . . . exalted those of low degree

This phrase sums up the theme of Mary's song. God uses what humanity often thinks of as useless. The ways of God are paradoxical. As we realize this again on this particular Sunday, we are of course being prepared for the sublime paradox of Mary's child. Everything about the birth will be paradoxical. That it should happen in a small village, that the child should be in a poor manger, that he should indeed be a fragile human child — all this is the paradox of God. As John Betjemen says wonderingly in his lovely poem "Christmas," "The Maker of the stars and sea, become a child on earth for me?" We must remember this always. God's ways are not our ways. Our way of judging someone, our way of assigning value and precedence, are simply not God's. Therefore we must be most careful about our facility for accepting and rejecting, for assigning importance to this and irrelevance to that. We may in God's judgement be utterly mistaken. Christmas, among many other things it does, humbles our systems of human judgement and assessment.

Psalm

Just as Micah mentioned that God's people can feel at times "lost and given up," so the psalm echoes this. It is as if God has moved some distance from humanity. There is a sense of shadow rather than light, of absence rather than presence, of loneliness rather than companionship. That can indeed be true for humanity as a whole in certain periods of history, for whole cultures, for an individual at various times in one's life. The reason the psalm is sung or said today is that we are on the edge of the event which promises God's presence in our humanity in a way nothing else could. God is about to become companion of our humanity, living our humanity out in daily life.

Christmas — at Midnight

Isaiah 52.7–10
Hebrews 1.1–12
John 1.1–14
Psalm 98

Theme All scriptures on this night centre around the birth of Our Lord. All are lyrical passages expressing deep mystery. We hear Isaiah speaking of a return from exile, a renewed people, a promise and a future. All are images of the promises which are ours from the holy birth (Isaiah). The writer of Hebrews reaches for a succession of cosmic images to express the uniqueness of Christ and the eternal nature of God (Hebrews). John also uses cosmic and universal images, trying to find language and thought large enough for what he believes to be true about this particular human life he has encountered (John).

First Reading *How beautiful upon the mountains are the feet of him who brings good tidings*

The circumstances of this homily place every word of the scriptures in the context of Our Lord's birth. However, it is important that this passage of Isaiah be given its own integrity apart from that event. We are still in exile in Babylon but, to the discerning mind of Isaiah, the way is being opened which will make return to Jerusalem possible. He is now committing all his energies to the nourishment of that hope among his people. He is so determined that his people will grasp this hope and act on it that he wishes them to think of return as if it had already taken place. Very often in a winter starved for snow one will see bumper stickers which say "Think Snow." In a sense Isaiah is employing a similar device. He is saying to Israel "Think Return." Notice how vividly he speaks of some things as if they already existed.

> *Your God reigns*

God does not seem to reign in their present situation. They are in exile, powerless under a great empire. But Isaiah wants them to realize that God ultimately reigns even though it is not now obvious.

> *Your watchmen lift up their voice . . .*
> *they sing for joy . . . they see the return*
> *of the Lord to Zion*

Do they actually see it? Of course not. But Isaiah is asking them to dream that these things are so, that they can hear the watchman sing on the walls of their own city, that they see the lines of the great caravans emigrating back to the open gates of that distant city on a hill.

> *Break forth together into singing, you*
> *waste places of Jerusalem*

Isaiah is realistic. He knows that by this time Jerusalem is largely a wasteland. But he wants them to envision that wasteland as already restored. So what can these things say to us on a Christian midnight in the late twentieth century? A great deal. What can particularly address us is the realization of Isaiah, that it was all important for his people *to dream the future into the present.*

Jurgen Moltmann says that we have almost forgotten that there are two words for the future. One is *futurum,* the other *adventus. Futurum,* he says, is the future we get by all our futurizing techniques — the poll, the survey, the projecting of present trends, the computerizing of all resulting data. That, says Moltmann is "the future of social calculation." But there also exists, he says, the kind of future we mean by the old word *adventus,* the future coming towards us, open with infinite possibilities. That he calls "the future of ethical anticipation." That future is possible when we begin to think through what we responsibly wish for ourselves or our family or our country or our world. It is not just an idle dreaming. It is an envisioning of the future which in turn can inspire and empower us in the present situation to work for the fulfilment of what we dream. In this century we are seeing what happens when a people is possessed by the vision of a radically different future. No sacrifice is too great. No attempt at stamping out the vision succeeds. Very ordinary people with primitive resources begin to successfully resist huge, technically equipped armies. The dream becomes itself an impervious armour. It empowers. That is the essential truth which Isaiah instinctively knew. A further factor which in Isaiah's case is immensely empowering is his conviction that this dream he possesses for his people is also the dream in the mind of God!

We ourselves as late-twentieth-century, Western people are in our own kind of exile or captivity. We are captive to many things. There will be different opinions about what those things are. We are certainly captive to the weapons we have ourselves formed, and we are desperately trying to get out of that mutual prison. We are captive to some of the wonderful new techniques we have discovered in medicine, captive in the sense that they face us with seemingly unanswerable dilemmas. We are captive to much materialism. We may be becoming willing captives to an inexhaustible flood of television options which can, if we wish, take a major portion of our waking lives. The list of our captivities is longer, but these will suffice as examples. What dreaming do we need to do about a future world?

At the heart of all this on this particular night is the Christ Child. That birth is the embodiment of the truth that God — new-creating, option-forming, future-opening — can always enter history. As a Christian, what dream do I think God is dreaming of the future? Am I prepared to ally myself with such a dream, giving my prayers and my energy and the best of myself to it, whether that be in the way I try to bring up a family or the way I try to function professionally or the way I participate in the life of the community? How can I become one who brings good tidings, who publishes peace (v 7)? Does my way of life communicate the fact that for me "God reigns" (v 7)? What "waste places" in the life of my city (my Jerusalem) am I prepared to do something about (v 9)? These are ways in which this passage can, I think, be used helpfully.

Second Reading *God spoke of old . . . but in these last days*

This is one of these magnificent passages set against a backdrop of the whole of time and space. In this it is like such passages as the eighth chapter of Romans, the first chapter of Colossians, and the first chapter of John's gospel. The writer is trying to get across a vast cosmic insight about the way in which the creating God works.

A Son, whom he appointed heir of all things, through whom also he created the world

Scriptures like this give the lie to the often repeated statement that it is Paul who has transformed a simple Galilean carpenter into a universal Saviour. This voice is certainly not Paul, and there is no doubt from these words that Christians even at this very early stage were placing Jesus Christ in a fundamentally different category from any great ones before him. The latter half of this scripture is saying categorically that somehow, within the full humanity of this person, there was also present that mysterious principle of life which we call the second person of the Trinity. To try to explain that in a homily on this particular night is self-defeating. The main thing is to communicate the mystery and the majesty of this. After all, it is precisely this undefinable and elusive mystery which gives this feast its real glory and power. Christmas has never been about the birth of just another child. It has, and will always, haunt the human consciousness because of the question which comes to us as we stand at the manger. That question eternally is, What child is this?

> *He reflects the glory of God . . . the very stamp of his nature . . . upholding the universe . . . superior to angels*

Each phrase, magnificent and awe inspiring, hammers home the ultimacy with which Jesus Christ is regarded. The whole of the rest of the passage is a series of images by which to do this, to make sure that Jesus Christ is seen as "anointed beyond [his] comrades" [v 9].

> *Thou, Lord, didst found the earth in the beginning . . . thou remainest . . . they will be changed . . . thou art the same*

The writer is at pains to say that this birth, this coming into history of the second person of the

Godhead, does not change the nature of God. God is not diminished or made less ultimate or less universal. Even to speak like this is to use groping and inadequate language where, in fact, all language is groping and inadequate! This is one of the truly great biblical expressions of the majesty of God. If any words or images can at all express it, these few lines do. Anselm of Canterbury once said that "God is that than which no greater can exist." These verses of Hebrews are a kind of hymn around that theme. These images of divine glory are most important today because of what they say to our contemporary fears about the dissolution of the world by our own enmities and our own inventions. We need to be reminded that, even though we most certainly must acknowledge the terrible and immediate reality of the threat to our world, God is not crouched in some corner of the universe trembling before our newly acquired human might! We may imagine the great love of God trembling on our account, having given us the gift of freedom to decide the fate of the human story. But that is very different from thinking of God as somehow grown lesser because of our human powers.

Third Reading   *In the beginning was the Word*

If by using the word *Word* John is trying to employ a familiar concept of his time to express what he wants to say about Jesus, then how do we express that same thing today in an understandable way? I would suggest that the following does not betray John's meaning.

As he begins to write about Jesus, he asks himself what device he can use to reach his readers. He remembers that there is a very ancient belief that at the heart of the universe there exists what is called the "Logos" or the "Word." This Word is the creative force God uses when God wishes to create. There is a fundamental difference about this Word and any human words we can use. When we use the word *star* we bring into being only the concept of a star. When

God speaks the divine Word *star*, there is a star! This Word is always waiting to be spoken, always waiting to be set to work by God to bring into being what God "says," always waiting to be made again and again the creating instrument or principle of God. God, John tells us, decides to bring into being ultimate humanity in a human life. In Jesus that Word begins to live in human flesh. The eternal Word enters time and space. It occupies human flesh. It becomes human. That, says John, is the awe-inspiring and almost inexpressible reality we face when we encounter Jesus Christ.

> *There was a man sent from God*

But not only John. There have been many lesser "words" sent by God in the voices of many men and women. Look back at the opening lines of the Hebrews passage. God has spoken in many voices. All of them were by way of preparation for this ultimate communication. In their various groping ways they "came to bear witness to the light."

> *The true light that enlightens every man*

A helpful image to delineate the gulf between Our Lord and others might be this: if other men and women have been, and indeed are, lamps or lights in the world, Our Lord is not merely another such light but rather the source of all those various lights.

> *The world knew him not . . . his own people received him not*

This sentence can so easily slide by in its total familiarity. It is expressing an essential element in the human tragedy. Our flawed and sinful humanity is capable of encountering the Good while being unable to recognize it. We are in fact capable of destroying it. We are capable of killing peace in the world. We are capable of killing someone else's genuine love. We are capable of closing our lives to God. But we are also capable of doing something else. . .

> *To all who received him, who believed . . . he gave power to become children of God*

We are capable of receiving Our Lord as indeed Lord of our lives. To do that is to receive power. Notice it is not for a moment understood in terms of personal, self-centred, exploiting power. We are given the power to give our allegiance to another. This is a paradoxical description of power. Yet the power to give ourselves to another is perhaps the most valuable and rewarding power in relationships. Many cannot give themselves to another, even when they wish to. The higher the reality to which we give ourselves, the greater the spiritual benefits we receive. The degree to which I can give myself to Jesus Christ is the measure of how much his Spirit enters and directs my life, empowering me to serve him.

> *The Word became flesh and dwelt among us*

These eight words contain the core claim of Christian faith. They are the whole heart of this season. Without this truth the lights, the trees, the carols, the gift giving, all become something else, something still beautiful and desirable and well-intentioned, but lesser and rather empty. There are some lines of John Betjeman which express this perfectly.

> And is it true? And is it true,
> This most tremendous tale of all,
> Seen in a stained-glass window's hue,
> A Baby in an ox's stall?
> The Maker of the stars and sea
> Become a Child on earth for me?
>
> . . . .
>
> No love that in a family dwells,
> No carolling in frosty air,
> Nor all the steeple-shaking bells
> Can with this single Truth compare —
> That God was Man in Palestine
> And lives today in Bread and Wine.

If one did no more in this midnight eucharist than quote these lines, one would have preached the Good News of God in Christ more than adequately.

Psalm

Think of the images of this psalm in terms of what we wish to express about this season of Christmas. The Lord is victor. What victory is here? In what sense does Our Lord's birth show righteousness (v 3)? What joy is here (v 5)? What have the sea, the hills, the rivers, the lands (vv 8,9) got to do with this birth? In what sense does the fact that God has entered human history change the way we think about the relationship of the human with the rest of creation? If God is really within our humanity, are we not responsible for it all? In the final verse we sing of righteousness, judgement, and equity or justice. Once again we are not allowed to forget the commitment of God to these things. Millions of Christians maintain that these things are political and sociological intrusions in the Good News of Our Lord. But even on this very night we are reminded otherwise!

First Sunday after Christmas

1 Samuel 2.18-20,26
Colossians 3.12–17
Luke 2.41–52
Psalm 111

Theme In all the scriptures there is an element of self-giving to God. The boy Samuel, received by his mother as an answer to her prayers, is returned to the service of God and is already being formed for his lifetime role (Samuel). Paul, writing to a Christian community, asks for no less than the offering of their inner and outer life, their thought and their action, to God (Colossians). In the single episode we have from Our Lord's youth, we see him seeking out the courts of the Lord and finding there the focus for his thought and energies (Luke).

First Reading

This passage of the Old Testament provides an intriguing mirror-like reflection of the gospel theme. All the elements of the early scenes in Our Lord's life are here. First there is the theme of childhood. Then in each story there is the common setting of a temple. In the old priest Eli who meets Hannah, there is a hint of the old man Simeon who will meet Mary. Each utters prophetic words to a couple about the future. Finally, the last words of this passage are borrowed presumably centuries later by Luke, to describe Our Lord as a child. This is obviously why the compilers of the lectionary selected it.

> *Samuel was ministering before the Lord,*
> *a boy girded with a linen ephod*

If we wish to use this passage for homilizing pastorally, how might we do so? The image of the child Samuel calls to mind a young server in today's church, carrying the vessels of the eucharist from the credence table to the altar, lighting the candles, etc. That image raises the whole question of the participation of children in worship. It may be one of the problems Anglican congregations must struggle with in the 1980s and 1990s. As I write, it is a very serious issue in many parish churches, and it arises from the acknowledged fact that the decision to have children present radically alters the way of our worship. No longer can it be the quiet, cerebral, dignified order most adults of today grew up with. Instead the service must be familial, flexible, to some degree noisier. The homily will have to be shorter than earlier decades demanded. If children are to be welcomed to receiving the bread and wine of the eucharist, then further acceptance on the part of adults is necessary. There will have to be understanding of the fact that, because a child does not show the traditional adult reverence for the act of receiving, this does not mean the child is in any way irreverent. To say these few things is not to name all the issues involved in the decision to include children in worship.

> *His mother . . . went up with her*
> *husband to offer the yearly sacrifice*

The parents of Samuel coming each year to the Temple can be used as an image of an eternally important reality in family life. The spiritual development of a child must be supported by the parents' example. A child cannot merely be directed to church by parents who themselves do not worship. A child will instinctively know what is and what is not significant for its parents' lives. Even in later teen years, when a young person is going through a very natural stage of rejecting parental stances, if there has been regular parental participation in worship, and if there is a good strong bonding in the family in spite of all normal teen rebellion, the chances are all for that young person returning to participation in worship in the years to come. The faithful support of Samuel's parents can legitimately be used as a basis for such reflection. The fact that they came only once a year arises out of the circumstances of travel and resources in a very different world. Between those special visits to the house of the Lord at Shiloh, there would have been their regular participation in worship in their own region at Ramah, where Elkanah had his own liturgical duties to perform.

Samuel was ministering . . . Eli would bless

In the child and the aging man we have eternal images of the church's life. There is the church that is linked to the past, and the church within it which is struggling to be born. To say this does not in the least dismiss the past as without value. It has immense value. But this eternal struggle is particularly sharp in these present years.

The loan which she lent to the Lord

The fact that Samuel is the firstborn of this couple, yet is given by them for service at Shiloh, can be used homiletically to reflect about the nature of giving in a Christian's life. One of the hardest truths to get across in contemporary stewardship issues is that worthwhile giving must be a decision taken before other financial decisions are made, not after they have all been made! True stewardship giving, which recognizes that all we possess belongs to God, is taken "off the top." It then becomes, to revert to the image of this passage, a giving of our firstborn. Because we are reflecting on these things in the days immediately after the celebration of Our Lord's birth, all of the above themes can be linked with that birth.

When we are speaking of children and worship, we may wish to cite the evidence to show that, even as a child, Our Lord was capable of intimations of God's presence. We can so easily underestimate the sensitivity of a child to God's presence, merely because the child is not exhibiting an adult seriousness in worship. As we reflect about parental support, we may wish to point out that Our Lord's early attitudes must have sprung from the deep love and support of both Mary and Joseph in quiet, ongoing ways never mentioned in the Gospels. As we reflect about Samuel being a costly gift of the firstborn child, we can see obvious links to the gift of Mary to the world and the later total self-giving of Our Lord.

Second Reading   *Put on then, as God's chosen ones*

Here is one of those moments when Paul does some dreaming, not idle day-dreaming but serious envisioning of what the Christian community might and can be. There follows a kind of word portrait of what a Christian community is called to be.

Holy and beloved

Does the degree to which we are capable of thinking of one another as holy measure the degree to which we can love one another? There is an old story of an abbot whose monastery was not doing very well.

The monks were dispirited and there was constant bickering. He had a friend in the nearby town, an old rabbi to whom he went to share his troubles. On this occasion he got very little satisfaction. The old rabbi seemed to be half listening. The abbot left rather disgruntled. Just as he was going the old rabbi called after him. "By the way, always remember that one of you may be the Messiah." The abbot could make no sense of the remark. However, he relayed it to the others on his return. Time went by. The thought refused to die. If the person you are with might be the Messiah, then you think twice how you treat that person. Attitudes began to change. Soon relationships in the abbey were transformed; its life became vibrant and creative. Nothing was ever the same again.

> *Compassion, kindness, lowliness, meekness, and patience*

There is nothing new here. These are the eternal ingredients required for human community. They are as necessary, and as elusive, in this century as in Paul's time. They are the marks of the human personality where the tyranny of the self has been broken and the focus is no longer on itself but on the other, the neighbour.

> *If one has a complaint against another, forgiving each other; as the Lord has forgiven you, so you also must forgive*

Here, as in the Lord's Prayer, we are reminded that to be a forgiving person we must realize that we ourselves have been forgiven. It may help to use the word *accepted*. As God has accepted me, in spite of what I am, so I am called to accept others in spite of what they are. This is an ingredient in human relationships without which community is impossible.

> *Put on love, which binds everything*
> *together in perfect harmony*

That thought never leaves Paul. It says a great deal for the quality of his relationship with Our Lord that he is haunted by a depth of love so deep that he has to resort to lyrical language to express it (as he does writing to the Corinthian community at another time). Even here in this short phrase he becomes lyrical. Obviously, to have this depth of commitment to the concept of love, he must have experienced it himself. None of us can speak of love or commend it to others if we have not ourselves become aware that we have received great love.

> *Let the peace of Christ rule in your*
> *hearts, to which indeed you were called*
> *in the one body*

Peace and unity — they occur together so often in the early Christian experience! Today in those congregations where the exchange of peace has become accepted practice, it has become a vehicle of unity. As we are all perfectly aware, the same practice can in some congregations be a bone of contention. Sad though this be, it may be necessary to decide that the time is not yet right for that congregation to express itself in this way. Sometimes there can be a period where the exchange of the peace is quietly and gently commended to the congregation by the practice of it among the clergy and those immediately involved in leading worship — readers, choir, those administering bread and wine as laity.

> *Let the word . . . dwell in you richly*

One notices the phrase "dwell in you." If there is a single most necessary task for late twentieth-century mainline Christian traditions, it is to renew the relationship of people with the Bible. Without an overall acquaintance with the great themes and images of scripture, much worship is weakened and rendered ineffective. It will not be enough to communicate a mere intellectual knowledge of the Bible. We must have a relationship with it by which it becomes for us a book whose places are not merely far away and in a long-ago time, but localities in the inner geography of our own lives. Bethlehem must become the centre where things come to birth in us, Gethsemane the region where we come to grips with our deepest challenges, Jerusalem the society we seek to bring into being, the Ark the symbol of our own planet bearing its teeming lifeforms. We need to recapture that capacity to read the Bible in a many-levelled way.

What we have in this passage is a description of an ideal Christian community. We might list its attributes again. Paul asks that it be a caring community (v 12); a forgiving community (v 13); a loving community (v 14); a community where unity is sought (v 15); a community committed to sacred scripture and to worship (v 16), a community of enthusiastic service motivated by its commitment to Jesus as Lord (v 17).

Third Reading *When he was twelve years old*

Notice how twelve years is dealt with between verse 40 and verse 41. The implication is that in those twelve years there was the normal growing up of a child to his youth. After this episode another eighteen years will be dealt with in the same way, again the implication being that Jesus participated in the ongoing normal life of a Galilean of his time. The efforts of the human imagination to fill these missing years is never-ending. At one end of the scale is the rather gentle and lovely book of John Oxenham's entitled *The Hidden Years*. At the other is the richly esoteric material which takes Jesus to remote parts of the planet, where he learns mysteries and secrets from various great men of wisdom. (Some of these now venerable scenarios are advertised as "New Age" in contemporary magazines!) Such material misses the whole thrust of the Bible which insists again and again that God comes in the everyday and the seemingly ordinary. We do not have to substitute exotic journeys across the planet in place of the roads of Galilee. If Jesus did journey in search of various sources of wisdom, he certainly does not communicate what he discovered in the convoluted languages and images used by some contemporary "new age" prophets and mystics!

> *The boy Jesus stayed behind in
> Jerusalem. His parents did not know it*

This episode is often spoken of as if the child Jesus got lost in Jerusalem. Scripture does not support that. There is at very least a suggestion of a conscious decision on the part of the youth. He was not "left" behind. He "stayed" behind. Likewise he quite obviously did not tell his parents. In other words, Jesus in the first flush of newly gained youth seems to have been as healthily oblivious as most young people to the cost of his decisions on the nerves and patience of parents! One of the statements of youth most calculated to cause parental despair is the universal "But Dad (or Mum), what were you worried about?" Later on in life, of course, the youth finds out, when he or she has children!

Why does he or she do it? For the same reason that this sort of thing will be done in families to the end of time, even in families where there are good communications and close relationships. There comes a time when we must see if we can fly a bit on our own. Most of us at that stage in life are ready to take some risks. We are ready to risk testing the relationship. It usually has got nothing to do with our love for a parent or parents. Recriminations such as "The fact that you would do that proves you don't really love us" are quite incomprehensible to a young person, simply because he or she does not think in those categories. We are watching Our Lord taking a most normal step in the human journey.

After three days they found him

We might now reflect on the costliness of parental responsibility. Many of us will know the slowly growing fears which lurk on the edge of the mind when we begin the search for a missing young person. We know how those peripheral fears move quickly to the centre of our being as each hour goes by. We know the strange mixture of rage and relief when a familiar face is seen.

One could also choose to reflect on the costliness of all real love; all genuine love involves self-sacrifice. Or one could use this scripture to speak of the search of each one of us for Jesus Christ. Most of us search for him in a city environment. Many who once knew him and lost him for some years are seeking for him again in various ways.

Finally, there is a whole other level of meaning in this scripture if we look at the rich symbolism for Christians in the phrase "three days." At the very heart of the Christian good news is the fact that Our Lord's disciples moved through the agony of the cross and "after three days they found him."

They did not understand the saying which he spoke to them

Loving across the generations often means continuing to love while not understanding what exactly is going on. Such love requires a great deal of trust in a parent.

> *He went down with them and came to Nazareth*

But from what we know ourselves of life, the youth who returned to Nazareth was not quite the same person who had left it a short time before. There had been all-important change and growth. The horizons of his world had rolled back. He had caught a glimpse of something that would now haunt him. He had heard a kind of music within himself that would echo for years to come. So it often goes in human experience. Something will happen on a single occasion. Sometimes the occasion is sought but sometimes not. It will leave a deep impression, but for various reasons it is not possible to continue in its presence. Like Our Lord, we must return to another place. The incident seems closed, the effect over, the chapter closed. But it is not so. Quietly, perhaps totally unconsciously, the memory works its will in the life of the person until it emerges in some life-changing way at another time.

> *His mother kept all these things in her heart*

One gets from this glimpse of Our Lord's mother a hint of great serenity and inner security. It does not seem to distress her that she cannot understand all that is going on. She doesn't try to wrestle answers from the mystery. She is prepared to live with it for at least a while. Being human she will not be able to live with it for ever. There will be obvious moments of hurt and disappointment and doubt. But for now she is ready to let be. We need to know when such times are here for us, times to refrain from insisting on answers, for the simple reason that there probably isn't one!

Psalm

As is true of many psalms, these verses are a portrait of God, painted in swift, vivid strokes delineating the attributes of God's nature. For the psalmist God is majestic, righteous, gracious, compassionate, nurturing (v 5), faithful, just, truthful, dependable (v 8), redemptive, awesome. To reflect on these properties of God is the core of all human attempts at wisdom. A short homily on this psalm might consist of a simple clarification of each one of these properties of God.

The Baptism of the Lord, Proper 1

Isaiah 61.1–4
Acts 8.14–17
Luke 3.15–17, 21–22
Psalm 29

Theme All the images of this season suggest a search for an ever-widening experience of what Our Lord's life and ministry mean. That search is ours if we choose. As we hear Isaiah speak of the servant's sense of mission, we can identify with that as being a call to us (Isaiah). As we see those in Samaria receive the Holy Spirit, we must ask what that means for our own lives (Acts). As we stand in the wilderness with John and discover Jesus among the crowd, we realize his presence in the contemporary wilderness (Luke).

First Reading *The spirit of the Lord God is upon me*

We cannot emphasize too often that a statement such as this is not some distant specialized statement about a supremely gifted man of God centuries ago. When a Christian reads this passage today, he or she must realize that the word of God directly addresses him or her. If the water of baptism has been poured over my life, then the Spirit of the Lord is indeed upon me. In fact we can go further. The Spirit of the Lord may be calling me as an adult towards baptism. If we really believe the role of the Holy Spirit in creation, then that same Spirit is upon me by virtue of my being part of God's creation. That the Holy Spirit of God is upon each one of us is totally beyond doubt!

The Lord has anointed me

If we have been baptized, then that has been our anointing. We are once again called, having already been called by our very creation. There seem to be three great moments of such calling. Our very creation calls us to God's service. Our baptism reiterates the call to serve God in terms of Jesus Christ. Perhaps the third is that mysterious moment or perhaps period in our lives when something moves us to respond consciously and intentionally. We realize our having been called, and we answer with a resounding yes!

To bring good tidings to the afflicted

What can that mean for us? Does it point to something immediate? Is there someone whom we have neglected to contact who needs the good tidings that we care for and think of them? This passage may mean a very simple thing for us, something like writing a card or lifting the phone or making a visit. It may mean something very different. It may suggest involving ourselves with those who work among the many in society who are in some way afflicted. Is there a group we know of who are involved in some work of social responsibility? Sometimes we are afraid of involving ourselves in such ways, because we feel we do not have any particular "good tidings" to bring to anyone in affliction. But for such people the good tidings are not in anything we say, but in the mere fact that we act in a caring way.

> *He has sent me to bind up the brokenhearted*

Notice that God has sent "me." Binding up the brokenhearted is not something awaiting the attention of some vague group who are "qualified specialists." We do not have to have a degree in "binding up the brokenhearted." We come across this illusion very often. Most men and women who are for many and various reasons brokenhearted do not need complicated and professional techniques to repair their brokenness. Many of us in such circumstances need only to know that we are loved and cared for.

> *To proclaim liberty to the captives*

There are so many kinds of captives. There are those who are literally captive. All over the world there are men and women unjustly made captive in repressive regimes. We might wish to give our time and our gifts to such a work as that of Amnesty International. There are those who wish to do a human and simple thing like unite their families, but who cannot do so because of barriers erected between countries. Many Jewish families in the Soviet Union are separated by such barriers. We may wish to voice our support by such simple but effective means as writing a letter to local Soviet embassies. All such personally written letters are significant to governments for their assessment of world opinion.

> *To proclaim the year of the Lord's favour, and the day of vengeance of our God*

Notice the balance. God affirms our humanity but also judges us. We are favoured creatures but we are also responsible beings. We are accountable to God.

We must accept the consequences of our actions and decisions. The Bible is not saying that God is a vengeful God in the sense that human beings are vengeful. It is saying that we as free beings bring upon ourselves consequences which God by God's very nature must allow. Our very freedom under God demands that.

> *To grant to those who mourn . . . a garland . . . the oil of gladness . . . the mantle of praise*

We can be in mourning for someone who has died, but there are many other ways in which we can be grieving. Loneliness and homesickness are such, as indeed they must have been for some of the people Isaiah was addressing here. The end of a marriage in divorce or separation. The facing of retirement. A youngest child's leaving home. We mourn at many times and in many ways. What can it mean in those many circumstances for us to give another person a garland, the oil of gladness, the mantle of praise? Consider this last image, the mantle of praise. Perhaps someone is mourning after some loss or failure which has cost dearly in terms of self-esteem and self-image. Such people are desperately trying to win this back in a new situation. They are fearful and fragile, wondering if they can take hold of life again. In such a situation praise given at the right moment and in the right way can be transforming. It has become well known in recent years that the single most neglected act in the workplace is the giving of deserved praise. The "mantle of praise" can do wonders for us all when we are of "faint spirit."

> *They shall build up the ancient ruins . . . former devastations . . . ruined cities*

In this passage we can hear about the many opportunities of ministry which are ours for the doing. We may do them as individuals or we may do them among others in community or in organizations. The achievements of any of our ministeries will be in terms of these images which Isaiah uses. We will be builders. We may be building up other men and women individually. We may be building the quality of life in a community or in another part of our society. We may be building the life of our church. The point is that to choose a stance of ministry in our lives is to become a builder for God. The deep and subtle reward for such ministry of building is that we discover ourselves being built at the same time. We ourselves are often the "ruin" and the "city" and the "devastation" being built. Many men or women who felt their lives to be in ruins and devastated have found their lives rebuilt by offering themselves for ministry among other people even in very simple ways.

Second Reading *When the apostles at Jerusalem heard that Samaria had received the word of God*

It is easy to miss the significant change in mindset shown here. For anyone in Jerusalem to believe for a moment or even to care that the word of God had appeared in any way in Samaria would have previously been unthinkable. Samaria was regarded as beyond consideration by all the traditions in which these men, now apostles of Jesus, had been raised. The fact that they now have this concern for Samaria is in itself an indication of the vast changes already taking place within them because of their relationship with Jesus Christ. What can this scripture say to us? What is "Samaria" for us? What issues, situations, aspects of life, disciplines, questions, challenges, do we too easily discount as being possible ministry for us? Where is there a word of God for us in today's life sciences?

In our relationships with men and women who have AIDS? In the various political issues of our times? All of these can so easily be a "Samaria", an area which seems not relevant to faith and in some way outside the word of God.

> *They sent to them Peter and John, who came down and prayed for them that they might receive the Holy Spirit*

Continuing the above thought we might ask this question. What parts of ourselves are we ready to send into those "Samarias," those neglected or discounted areas which seem only distantly connected with Christian faith? To what extent are we prepared to make such things the matter of our prayer? To what extent are we prepared to see them as the domain of the Holy Spirit?

> *Then they laid their hands on them and they received the Holy Spirit*

There are many areas of life on which we have not "laid hands." We have not reached out to them and touched them fully and willingly. That applies to certain people in our lives, to certain areas of our own lives, to certain tasks we have never really grappled with. There may be many reasons for our not laying hands on these things. There may be fear or guilt or previous hurts. But until, with God's help, we lay hands upon them and truly grasp them, we shall not experience in them the presence of the Holy Spirit for ourselves, nor shall we be able ourselves to bring to them the Holy Spirit.

Third Reading *As the people were in expectation, and all men questioned in their hearts concerning John, whether perhaps he were the Christ*

Two aspects of this verse are immediately applicable to our situation today. It is very obvious that people are now "in expectation" and that all men and women have many questions about almost everything in contemporary experience. Can we attempt to define what being "in expectation" today might mean?

There is a realization among many that at the very least the future must be radically different from the past if it is to be a human future. We are in expectation that our relationship with the environment around us will have to change. We are in expectation that the economic systems of our world will have to be altered if a whole new generation is to find employment. We are in expectation that the present relationship of uneasy truce between the two great superpowers cannot forever depend on what is suitably called Mutually Assured Destruction (MAD). In these and many other matters we are a generation in expectation.

All men questioned in their hearts

By the very nature of the times in which we live, we must accept the fact of there being many more questions than answers. We are in so many ways striking out into unknown territory, particularly in the life sciences. We are wrestling to understand our own humanity, and we do not know what shall be. The image in the Bible which unerringly describes such a state is that of being in the wilderness. The wilderness is the place of many questions and few answers. It is not without significance that John the Baptist chooses the wilderness, or at least the edge of it, in which to encounter his listeners from the city. We are all these days the people of "the city." The city is the place of answers rather than questions; at least it is the place where there are supposed to be answers, where we expect them. The city is where there are supposed to be the resources to deal with anything. The city is where we feel in control. The city is the opposite of the wilderness. That is why there is a deep wisdom and power in John's decision to hurl his chilling message to the "city" from the grimness of the "wilderness."

> *He who is mightier than I is coming*

For John there is a sense of one coming almost immediately. The expectation of a specific national Messiah was very vivid for his hearers. Such an eventuality is as ready to our minds, unless we are among those Christians who feel that the return of Our Lord is near. That returning of Our Lord is, of course, a profound mystery. All we can be sure of is that creation belongs to God, and so its purpose in being also belongs to God. The consummation (or the ending or the crowning) of the universe is in the hand of God. What we believe as Christians is that, whatever the actuality of that consummation will be, we will discern in it those elements of love, new creation, and resurrection which we saw, and eternally see, in Our Lord.

> *He will baptize you with the Holy Spirit and with fire . . . clear his threshing floor . . . gather the wheat . . . chaff he will burn*

All the images are sobering and salutary. They speak of human will being deeply challenged by a higher will. They speak very clearly of our being accountable for our lives. They leave no doubt about there being consequences for human decisions and actions.

> *When Jesus also had been baptized and was praying . . . the Holy Spirit descended . . . a voice came*

The expected one is actually present, hidden among the listening crowd! But this is true of our experience too. What we expect and hope for is in some sense present if we are prepared to seek it among the "crowd" of our lives, the crowd of thoughts, pressures, temptations, responsibilities, desires, which are always milling about within and around us. We may well look to a coming of Our Lord at some future time, just as we remember his coming in a past time. But he comes in the present moment if we are prepared to discern his presence in the present situation, the present challenge. In such a moment the Holy Spirit can come into our experience. There can be a voice which identifies and validates and affirms us.

Psalm

Notice how the poet reaches out into every facet of human life to discern God's glory. All other "gods" (values? loyalties? lifestyles? commitments?) are to be given less standing than the ultimate God. The glory of God is to be discerned in worship (vv 2, 9). Glory is given to God in all the aspects of nature. The glory of God is seen in the search for peace among nations and within societies (v 11).

Second Sunday after Epiphany, Proper 2

Isaiah 62.1-5
1 Corinthians 12.1-11
John 2.1-11
Psalm 36.5-10

Theme All the scriptures express in some way the generosity of God. A people still reeling from the trauma of exile, feeling a terrible loss of self-esteem, are reassured that God delights in them as ever (Isaiah). Paul emphasizes that all gifts have their own particular value because all come from God (Corinthians). At the wedding where wine has run out, new wine is supplied in abundance (John).

First Reading *For Zion's sake I will not keep silent*

The prophet's task is to restore the morale of a shattered and exiled people. He must give them the will to rebuild a society, to believe again in the possibility of a future for themselves. Think how contemporary this passage would sound in modern Uganda, in some Central American countries, in Argentina — to name a few of the places where a society battered by terrible events is seeking to come together again and to rebuild. This reminds us that the Bible can speak most powerfully when its events can be seen in terms of present experience. Exile, social disintegration, and power struggles between deeply differing ideologies are not the present experience of most

North Americans. However, these are realities for millions of people elsewhere.

> *You shall be called by a new name*

This is precisely what has happened all over the world in the last few decades. Nation after nation has celebrated independence (however illogical and economically fragile that has seemed to us in the West) by changing a name very often given by colonizers. Instead, a name from their own history is taken, symbolizing the restoration of the life of that people.

> *You shall no more be termed Forsaken . . . Desolate . . . you shall be called My delight is in her*

In modern language we might say that it is necessary for a society's self-image to be changed from a sense of low self-worth, a sense of powerlessness, to a sense of possessing a role and a vocation.

> *Your land [shall be called] Married . . . so shall your sons marry you*

Which means that, instead of the people of the country being alienated from its institutions, they will be able to identify with (i.e., marry) its institutions, because for the first time they will regard those institutions and symbols as their own.

While all of the above is immensely relevant if this passage is read in a contemporary social situation which reflects it, the passage will not speak vividly in those terms to a Christian in the developed world. It may be possible to commend this scripture on a personal level in the following way.

> *For Zion's sake . . . for Jerusalem*

Let "Zion" be the inner citadel of our personal lives. As persons we know only too well that we can experience exile of many kinds. We can be deprived and separated from love, from hope, from everything that makes life worthwhile. That may happen through our own actions, through suffering, through many things. We may feel "forsaken and desolate" (v 4). But with God's help we can come to see that that is not the final reality about us. God has a role and a vocation for us. We are nothing less than a crown of beauty and a diadem in God's hand (v 3). In other words, God has a use for our gifts and abilities. God can and will use us. The deep sense of alienation in us can and often does change to a sense of reconciliation. The broken parts of us can come together again. It's as if we become "married" again to ourselves and to others and to God. In this way the passage can become a powerfully healing passage on a personal level.

Second Reading *Now concerning spiritual gifts*

Just as the previous passage of Isaiah was all about encouraging Israel to see itself as a gift to others rather than something cast off and useless, so this chapter is about our capacity to see the spiritual gifts we have.

No one speaking by the spirit of God ever says "Jesus be cursed!"

Paul was speaking to people who had abandoned demeaning and wildly emotional practices. They had not evaluated religious experience. Paul points out that having some deep religious experience is not in itself enough. We have to ask what kind of an experience it is, what quality of spirit we have encountered.

Varieties of gifts, but the same spirit

A very necessary corrective in contemporary Christian life. If we have had an all-consuming experience of the presence of Our Lord, it is always a temptation to feel that those who have not been given such an experience are somehow less than we are. We would be shocked to realize that this is what we are often communicating by our attitude. No gift of God is lesser or greater than another.

Varieties of service, but the same Lord

There are many functions in the Christian community. None are greater or lesser. They are merely different. There is a priesthood at the altar, but there is another kind of priesthood lived out in the downtown office and the hospital and the garage and the supermarket.

The same God who inspires them all in every one

The reasons that all gifts are on the same level and that all "varieties of service" are the same, is that the source of all of them is God. In that sense our gifts are not ours. They are gifts given to us which we then exercise. Because of this, there is no such thing as spiritual gifts and non-spiritual gifts. All are the gifts of God.

To each is given the manifestation of the Spirit for the common good

That is the sole reason why gifts are given. We live in a society where it is easy to begin to believe that our gifts are merely for self-advancement and self-fulfilment. Not so. Our gifts, if they are to be truly spiritual, are given for the common good. Paradoxically, if we remember this and use them in this way, we receive even greater self-fulfilment. We receive it, as we do so many of the things of God, not as something directly sought after but as an unexpected by-product as we offer ourselves to a particular good which is outside and around us.

The utterance of wisdom . . . the utterance of knowledge

Notice that there is a difference. Wisdom is the way we choose to live out the knowledge we possess. One can have much knowledge and live in a way that shows a great lack of wisdom.

To another faith

Notice that apparently faith is not a universal gift! We often lash ourselves for not having it, thinking that someone else most certainly has. We need to realize that most of us do not so much possess faith as search for it.

To another gifts of healing

Some most certainly have such a gift in many ways. Even in medical practice itself, all doctors have access to much the same knowledge and skills and resources, but some will be better healers than others by virtue of their essential, inner being. Other people will have the gift of healing relationships. Others will have the gift of healing psychic pain by their sensitivity and their counselling. Such people with various gifts of healing will achieve miracles. They will heal where we did not expect it or even dare hope for it.

To another prophecy

Whenever we are speaking with insight about God, an insight which we wish to use for God rather than for our own reputation for cleverness, then we are prophesying. People trying to get across to another some truth about God that they have come to know out of their own experience — they are prophesying.

The ability to distinguish between spirits

This is a most necessary gift in today's world. Around us are all sorts of spirits, from the most evil and destructive to the most sublime. Many people claim spiritual experiences. That does not guarantee that the experience is of the presence and beauty and love of God. People can be claimed by spirits that destroy them as persons. The greatest service we can do one another as Christians is to demand mutual responsibility for the spirituality by which we live.

Third Reading   *There was a marriage in Cana of Galilee*

This episode of Our Lord's life is brimming over with such depths of meaning and symbolism that we must choose one of the many ways of reflecting on it. Suppose we look at the marriage as an image of human life. Human experience is indeed a marriage of many things — joy and sorrow, pain and ecstasy, celebration and suffering. The marriage, then, is the totally varied scene of human experience. Cana is the human community.

Jesus was invited to the marriage

In the case of our own life, with its marriage of many contradictions — gifts and weaknesses, successes and failures, trust and betrayals — is Jesus an invited guest? Is Our Lord part of the process of our living, invited into the heart of it, welcomed and given hospitality?

The wine gave out

The wine at the wedding of human life does indeed give out, sometimes suddenly and without warning, sometimes unnoticed and gradually. By "the wine" we might mean all that is desirable and joyful in human experience. There are times when that stops. It can stop because of sudden disaster, because of loss of health, because of some action of another which affects our lives, which betrays and hurts. The wine of life can suddenly run out because of a death which affects us deeply. The wine of joy and celebration can run out of the marriage of life during an experience of depression. It is the mother of Our Lord who first realizes the situation. We have learned that in human life it is the feminine side of our nature which is most sensitive to changes in our life situation. It is the feminine which first becomes aware that "the wine" is running out.

Do whatever he tells you

Good advice for all of us when we are faced with the running out of life's "wine." It is important to remember that among our guests (i.e., within our lives) there is a guest who can be resource to us. We can go to that guest (to Our Lord) in prayer and acknowledge what has happened. Notice how starkly and simply the news is conveyed to Jesus. There is no tentative euphemistic language. Nobody says, "By the way, we may have a bit of a problem coming up here." Instead, reality is named. "They have no wine," Our Lord's mother says, directly and honestly. That is a good pattern for our prayer. It is most effective when it is totally honest and without pretending. The language of prayer needs to be honest to be effective.

Notice how frequently in the Bible good things begin to happen when men and women take responsibility for their actions by stating simply and almost brutally that they have sinned. Prayer can be powerful when we acknowledge reality. Lord, I have lost my nerve. Lord, I have betrayed my marriage. Lord, I am an alcoholic. Lord, I am deeply depressed. Such is the language of potentially healing prayer. It is the same powerful honesty as "they have no wine."

Jesus said to them, "Fill the jars with water"

When the wine of life runs out, in the sense in which we are using this term, then we have to use the resources to hand. If wine is the celebration of life — its gifts, its strengths, its joys — then water is the other side of life — its ordinariness, its flatness, its greyness at times. What Our Lord is saying to us in this story is that when we use these very realities we begin to make new wine! The very ordinariness of life can be the source of that which is more than ordinary. The "water" of life can be made into "wine," if Our Lord is indeed a guest in the "wedding" of our inner being.

Twenty or thirty gallons

The story is suggesting that it is even possible to find more new "wine" (i.e., new strengths, new possibilities, new resources) than we can possibly need or want!

You have kept the good wine until now

As the person at the wedding says this to Jesus, so Our Lord says this to us as a possibility for our experience. We may well arrive at a point in life when we feel that the wine has run out. It may, as we said, be a feeling of being aged. It may be a bout of depression. It may be new limitations from some sickness, the loss of a job, or the break-up of a relationship. There are endless ways in which the wine of life runs out! What Our Lord says to us is that there may be many unsuspected things from which, if we choose, we can make new wine, even to the point of discovering, much to our surprise, that the new wine is even better than the old. Sometimes that new wine has been enriched by our tears and our pain. The first wine of our life may have been bright and bubbly and sharp. The new wine and later wine of life can be rich and deep and mature.

Psalm

Notice the rich variety of images of God in these few lines. God as lover. God as the faithful one. God as righteous. God as just. God as saviour. God as refuge. God as the keeper of the well of life. God as light. Each one of these images is in itself a source of reflection.

Third Sunday after Epiphany, Proper 3

Nehemiah 8.1–4a, 5–6, 8–10
1 Corinthians 12.12–30
Luke 4.14–21
Psalm 19.7–14

Theme An element of vocation can be discerned in all the scriptures. A recovering nation hears the law read publicly to remind the people that they are to be loyal to their covenant with God (Nehemiah). Using the image of the human body Paul points to the necessity for each of us to offer our own gifts and to accept those of others in God's service (Corinthians). Our Lord, while expressing his own sense of vocation in the words of Isaiah, calls us to our vocation (Luke).

First Reading *All the people gathered*

The scene is a city still in the process of rebuilding. The people have returned from exile, and under the leadership of Nehemiah and Ezra the task of reestablishing the life of a nation goes on. It has been a brutal challenge and they have succeeded in the face of many obstacles, not least enemies in the surrounding territories. We are at the point when much of the physical work has been done. The walls of the city are once again in reasonable shape. Now the time comes to do rebuilding of another kind, the rebuilding of a society, the rebuilding of human lives, the rebuilding of mutually accepted standards which will make the future possible.

Ezra the scribe stood on a wooden pulpit

It is one of those vivid details which brings a scene alive. What is happening is very important. The walls are built; now the fabric of the society has to be strengthened. The law is going to be read, acknowledged, and enforced. It is not the beginning of a dictatorship but of a very authoritarian chapter of Israel's history. Notice the precise list of those other significant public figures who are given prominence at this moment. In modern terms the whole caucus has come together on this particular political policy! (Notice that all these names do not have to be read, according to the lectionary!) Notice too in verse 5 the solemnity of the occasion. Every nuance is milked for its effect.

They read from the book, from the law of God . . . and they gave the sense, so that the people understood

Not only was the law read in the original language but also it was translated into the more familiar Aramaic, so that nobody could plead incomprehension if they in any way broke the law. On the surface this seems a sacred event. Underneath it is also highly political. We have many equivalents in today's world, most, of course, carried out in secular terms. At a certain stage in the development of Maoism in mainland China, the compulsory reading of the Little Red Book of Chairman Mao — even the public reading of it in village squares to gatherings who had no choice but to listen — was a modern echo of this moment in Israel. In a much different way, so much is the new Canadian Charter of Rights intended to be the basis on which a society operates, that everybody needs to be aware of its terms.

Having said all this, how can we use it for homily? Are there times for "reading the book of the law" in various situations? We might think of family life and church life. There are times when families must gather to recognize the rules of the house. These rules must be accepted and obeyed if the home is to function. Do we do that? How important is it? In church, what emphasis do we place on the reading of the two great commandments or the reading of the ten commandments? Even when the ten commandments are within the lectionary readings, do we take the opportunity to point out how very much they are the basis of social existence as we know it? Usually in modern times society as a whole is only aware of the deep moral and legal underpinnings which make its life possible when some terrible event happens to either challenge or undermine those foundations. In our educational system, do children and youth get enough grounding in even the outlines of the constitutional framework of this society? Can we take it for granted to the extent we do at present?

> *This day is holy to the Lord your God;*
> *do not mourn or weep*

It is possible that the weeping was for joy that the law of the Lord was once again being proclaimed in Jerusalem. However, leadership was obviously anxious that the occasion be one of celebration. We might see here that, while law can be oppressive and tyrannical in the wrong hands (in such hands it can become the very opposite of law), at best it is very much a basis for celebration. Without it we could not function as a society. Much that we take totally for granted is possible only because of the underpinning of law in our society, the unsaid assumptions about its presence and its sanctions.

Another aspect of this episode which may be helpful for homily is that reading the law to the people sent a strong message that they were precisely that — a people. Today, in a society of very marked individualism, we also need that corrective. We need to be reminded of those things we hold in common, the things which make us a community rather than just a vast conglomerate of individuals. In contemporary liturgy the repeated use of the phrase "a people of God" has precisely this intention.

Second Reading   *For just as the body is one and has many members . . . so it is with Christ*

We are looking at one of Paul's truly great insights about Christian life and spirituality. Nothing could be more immediate and understandable than the image of the human body. We are conscious both of its variety and its unity. I have many parts, but I am also aware of a unified consciousness within and of them all, the mystery I refer to as "I." So with Christians. Each of us is a member of a body. The consciousness of Christ is at the heart of that body. The body itself is the body of Christ.

If the foot should say . . . if the ear should say . . . if the whole body were an eye

This whole passage — gentle, tasteful, tinged with slight humour yet unrelenting in its challenge to certain personal claims and postures — is a masterly image by which to teach. No wonder it has been used again and again down the Christian generations. There will always be the member of a group who thinks his or her gifts of most importance. There will always be the member who tries to take over the whole group (i.e., claim to be the whole body). There will always be the person who cannot see that, if you ignore people's gifts, the body or the group is very much the poorer.

> *The eye cannot say to the hand . . . nor again the head to the feet, "I have no need of you"*

Life is absolutely interdependant. People are interdependant. We dismiss each other only with the certainty of our own impoverishment.

> *The parts . . . which seem to be weaker are indispensable . . . [the] less honorable we invest with the greatest honor*

How very difficult that is in our culture. Those who are weak are indispensable. Does that show in our programming, our membership? Does it show in such a thing as our design of buildings for the handicapped? Yet Paul pulls us up short when he goes on to say that God has so composed the body, giving the *greater honour* to the inferior part! Do we really believe that to be true? Do we act as if it is? Do we run our organizations, even our churches, as if it were true? Yet here it is bluntly and clearly said in scripture.

> *That the members may have the same care for one another*

A beautiful and gentle statement of a great truth. We are only beginning to realize in our driven, competitive culture that we must care for ourselves (e.g. my brain, by the decisions it takes and the responsibilities it accepts, must care for the capacity of my heart to take the strain of those responsibilities). Not only that, but as members of a group or community we are to care for one another. Paul ends this section with a moving description of ultimate human community, one where if one suffers, all suffer, and if one is honoured, all are honoured. How does our Christian community fare if judged by that standard?

You are the body of Christ

It is a breathtaking statement. We have become too familiar with it. It should still take our breath away when we think about it. We, so terribly ordinary and flawed, you and me, the body of Christ! It's impossible. Yes, in human terms it is impossible, but the love of God in Christ has made it possible.

Are all apostles? . . . all prophets?

Thank heaven, no! If the church were totally composed of one kind of person and one kind of gift, it would be a frightful place. If it were centred around, and obsessed by, the unique value of one kind of gift, it would be useless. Paul makes this very clear, yet it is amazing we still find this temptation in the life of God's people.

Third Reading *Jesus returned in the power of the Spirit*

It is easy to miss a great spiritual truth here. Jesus has just come through trauma and challenge. He has made some huge decisions in very daunting circumstances. He has been alone in a wilderness in both a literal and an inner sense. He has been tired and hungry. Yet, in spite of all this, the scripture says that he returned in the power of the Spirit. We can assume, then, that walking with God's Spirit is not an experience merely of the quiet, relaxed, religious, pleasant times of our lives. There is no guarantee that our encounter with the Holy Spirit will be at those times. Our Lord's encounter with the Holy Spirit was in turmoil and decision making, doubt and danger. This teaches us something about our own potential experiences.

> *A report concerning him went out through all the surrounding country. He taught . . . being glorified by all*

It is obvious that the wilderness experience has, if anything, energized and focused Our Lord for his mission. That is sometimes our experience. A period in our lives may be most unpleasant, a seeming waste of time, a professional or personal detour and cul de sac. We emerge from it relieved that we have survived, only to find that the experience has released all sorts of new things in us, enriched us and energized us for the next stage of life.

> *He came to Nazareth, where he had been brought up*

It would have been perfectly understandable to postpone that difficult visit. Luke is typically sensitive to add "where he had been brought up." Our "Nazareth" is where we are known completely, including our past. Nazareth is the place where, for each of us, there is no place to hide, no place to put on a false appearance. In our Nazareth we are vulnerable. Jesus doesn't hesitate to go there.

> *He went to the synagogue, as his custom was*

Anyone who tries to portray Our Lord as a solitary mystic, intent on his own "inner journey," has a difficult time justifying that from sacred scripture. The evidence seems to point to the fact that Our Lord was a regular worshipper in the synagogues of his day. One is inclined to observe that, if the company of the ordinary folk of his day was good enough for him, then the ordinary folk of a parish church are surely good enough for us! There are self-styled Christians who think otherwise!

He stood up to read

A whimsical thought. Is this the original image for all lay reading? After all, Our Lord was, in our terms, a layman. It is easy to forget that. These days in church there are sometimes grumblings about the degree of lay participation being encouraged. It is salutary to realize that it all begins with Our Lord!

The Spirit of the Lord is upon me

I have often emphasized that any statement like this in scripture can be true of us who read it. As we listen to Our Lord, it may be worthwhile to ask ourselves to what extent the things we read apply to ourselves. If they do not, then what are the terms of our own Christian vocation?

> *To preach good news to the poor . . . proclaim release to the captives . . . sight to the blind . . . set at liberty those who are oppressed . . . proclaim . . . year of the Lord*

From Our Lord to us the words ring down the centuries, as they did that day down the centuries from Isaiah to Our Lord. Again and again they have called forth a sense of mission in men and women. They have been the womb of many movements of reform, even many revolutions. They have expressed the vision of a society of justice no less compelling because it can never be perfectly attained. They have become a kind of charter of the Christian commitment to social injustice. The supreme irony may be in the fact that time and time again Christians who act upon these words have been dismissed as radicals, dreamers, in our day even as Marxists, when all the time they have been made captive by the same vision that motivated their Lord. In Helder Camara's words: "When I gave the poor bread I was called a Saint. When I asked why the poor were poor I was called a Marxist."

Today this scripture has been fulfilled in your hearing

This scripture is being fulfilled in some part of the world in every age. Particularly in our time it would seem to be finding fulfilment in South and Central America and in southern Africa. We may be tempted to say that its fulfilment is exacting a tragically high price. But then we have only to read further into scripture to see that Our Lord's uttering of these words had its own tragically high price, which he himself paid and from which emerged great glory and endless new life.

Psalm

A reflection on the beauty of the law of God which buttresses all human life. Tribute is paid to its perfection, its sureness, its justice, its clarity, its purity, its essential and utter truth (vv 7–10). If such a law becomes the basis for personal living, it can give one's life a wholeness and an integrity which enable us to offer ourselves to God for his service.

Fourth Sunday after Epiphany, Proper 4

Jeremiah 1.4–10
1 Corinthians 13.1–13
Luke 4.21–30
Psalm 71.1–6

Theme All the scriptures speak of vocation and of our wrestling with the consequences of that. Jeremiah hears the call of God but feels totally inadequate in the face of it. (Jeremiah). In his description of God's demand that we make love our ultimate vocation, Paul speaks of it as something we must mature towards (Corinthians). Jesus' words at Nazareth elicit the all too frequent human response from people called to face challenging moral and ethical issues (Luke).

First Reading *The word of the Lord came to me saying*

It is easy to glance at a passage such as this and to presume that it is the experience of someone "in the Bible," someone long ago who somehow had a relationship and encounters with God totally unlike our experience. It is vital to rid ourselves of this illusion. The simple yet profound truth is that the word of the Lord comes to you and to me. At least it tries very hard to do so! Because we are late twentieth-century people, God probably has a very difficult time trying to get through to us. But the important point is that God's relationship and God's dealings with us do not change merely because centuries pass and cultures change. God is eternally God! When we realize this is so, we can begin to assume that God is trying to say a word to us, and then our task is to seek what the word or words might be. It is essential to remember this rather than to think of Jeremiah as special because he is "in the Bible." Jeremiah never knew he was "in the Bible"!

> *Before I formed you in the womb I knew you. . . I consecrated you. . . I appointed you*

Of course, all this will be shown to be true in a very special way for Jeremiah. After all, he is about to become a voice immortalized in sacred scripture. But the four things that Jeremiah hears from the word of the Lord are four things we very much need to hear about our own lives. It is true of everyone of us that God has formed us, that God is aware of our lives, that God has a purpose for our lives. God's hope for us is that we offer ourselves to his will and purpose for us. He has appointed us in the sense that there is a task for us to do.

> *I do not know how to speak . . . I am only a youth*

The Bible shows us this pattern very often. It is human nature to retreat from the call of God initially. There is an immediate sense of inadequacy. Moses feels it, Isaiah expresses it. Peter in his own simple way knows it in the boat on the lake. The first response of all of us is to retreat from the call to what God wants us to do. We have endless and perfectly good reasons. We cannot speak, we are not good enough, we simply could not attempt it, we know exactly the right other person to do the job. On and on our reasons go. Down deep there is also the feeling that, while God calls people "in the Bible" and maybe some great saints here and there, God is simply not going to do anything as unlikely as to call us! This is exactly what all the other people whom God called thought too!

I am with you to deliver you

Again and again in the record of scripture the response of God is repeated. The instinctive human refusal is challenged. Instead, something is offered, often some symbol or embodiment of God's grace. In Isaiah's vision it is a burning coal. With Moses it is his brother Aaron. To Jeremiah God offers divine grace and strength.

I have put my words in your mouth

What follows that statement to Jeremiah is rather awe-inspiring. With the grace of communication given to him, he will affect his society deeply. His influence will reach far beyond his own people. Here is an example of how seriously the Bible regards the power of the word, the power of communication. We have seen this often in world affairs. We have witnessed a Churchill change European history by the power of language, a Hitler cast a shadow over the same Europe by the same power. We are seeing in our lifetime the whole of human society being radically changed by television, again a form of communication. We are only beginning to recapture in today's church a sense of the key role of our own efforts to communicate the Christian faith among our people. In the lives of lay people we are only beginning to touch the possibilities of lay witness in quiet and natural ways in a world where millions of laity function and relate to one another.

Second Reading

We are now at one of the great high points of the whole New Testament. Some would say that outside the four Gospels this passage of Paul's is the "Everest" of the New Testament. Paul has been describing various gifts of the Spirit. At the end, or rather at the apex of that list, he places love.

> *If I speak in the tongues . . . have prophetic powers . . . understand all . . . have all faith . . . give away all I have . . . my body to be burned . . . but have not love, I gain nothing*

Here is a list of many other valid spiritual gifts. We might think of prophetic powers as insight. The list would then include spiritual insight, understanding, faith, generosity, self-sacrifice. Paul is in no sense belittling any single item. He is going further. He is saying that, fine as these things are, they all need to be tempered by the greatest gift which we call love. Without love spiritual insight can become judgemental, understanding can become a cold intellectualism, faith can become cerebral and even arrogant, generosity can become a patronizing of others and something of an ego trip. Self-sacrifice can become neurotic and self-congratulatory. All have to be tempered and refined by love.

> *Love bears all things, believes all things, hopes all things, endures all things*

When we say love bears all things, we do not mean that love lies down and allows itself to be walked on. Bearing all things and believing all things does not mean that love must be innocent and naive. Pushing back or responding to pressure or opposition is not necessarily unloving. Great love will sometimes choose to bear and endure things because it has decided realistically that this is its vocation in a particular set of circumstances. Great love will find it possible to go on hoping, not merely stubbornly or blindly, but with total awareness of the reality of the situation. It consciously chooses to hope. Hoping is seen as its present vocation. The love which Paul is talking about, the love seen in and lived out by Our Lord, is very far from weakness or sentimentality. It can be utterly gentle and yet strong as steel. Above all, it harbours no illusions about the reality of life. It is clear in its vision and in its thinking.

> *Love never ends . . . prophecies pass away . . . tongues cease . . . knowledge will pass away*

Everything changes. The brilliant and sometimes radical breakthroughs of one time become the established dogmas of another. The theories of one era become the dismissed fantasies of another. The emotional experiences of one stage of our lives become the embarrassing memories of later years. The acknowledged truths of one time become the discredited illusions of another. But our capacity to be human beings who can love and be loved is the measure of our humanity at all stages of life and at all periods of history.

> *When I was a child, I spoke . . . thought . . . reasoned like a child*

Life is about maturing, about a journey from childhood to adulthood, from innocence to sophistication. But the measure of our maturing is not only in gifts such as knowledge and reasoning and articulation. All of these can become merely self-serving. The true measure of our maturing is our capacity to give and to receive love.

> *Now we see in a mirror dimly, but then face to face. Now I know in part*

Love constantly reminds us that we do not understand everything in any given situation. We see through the blinkers of our own personality and assumptions. We have also learned the degree to which we project our subconscious attitudes on to others. We have learned the eternal presence of the subjective in all our dealings. The effect of such realizations can be to help us refrain from over-confident, judgemental stances.

Third Reading *Today this scripture has been fulfilled in your hearing*

This statement of Our Lord, made in that long-ago synagogue in Nazareth, is addressed to us whenever we read a passage of scripture. It is essential for us to ask of any scripture we read, Where is this true (fulfilled) in contemporary experience? This question transforms Bible reading from mere history reading to contemporary experience. Take this very episode. In today's Christian community (the synagogue) Our Lord has come again and made two transformations in us. He has placed before us the necessity of becoming serious about Bible study. He has also made us face those parts of the Bible which call us to special concern. It is as if Jesus had stood up among our worship gatherings and done this.

> *All spoke well of him, and wondered at his gracious words*

So far there is no unpleasant reaction even though Jesus has read from one of the most challenging chapters in the whole of the Hebrew scriptures. Likewise, in modern congregations people can listen quite placidly to a reading from the prophet Amos that is lashing out brutally at things which a great many people in the Western world take for granted. What has made this possible? It is chiefly a kind of envelope of sanctity about scripture which in turn becomes an envelope of unreality. It is also a result of the deep gulf formed in Western culture between spirituality and so-called "real life." We can hear the voice of a long-ago prophet rail against poverty and injustice, but somehow that is "biblical" poverty and injustice, as distinct from contemporary "real" poverty or injustice. Such "real" issues we feel to be the agenda of politics, law, the media. But something can happen to arouse people's feelings. We see this as we watch Our Lord in that synagogue.

> *Today this scripture has been fulfilled in your hearing*

Jesus begins to apply the scripture in a topical and contemporary way, thus ensuring a reaction. The same is true today in a like situation. Not until this is done will people make the link between religion and reality.

> *There were many widows in Israel in the days of Elijah . . . and there were many lepers in Israel in the time of the prophet Elisha*

Jesus takes two "news items" from the history of his listeners. In those two cases God seems to have acted for people outside Israel. In saying such a thing Jesus is presenting himself a liberal in terms of the contemporary nationalism of his time. He is challenging the idea that Israel is favoured in any particular way unless it earns that favour. For obvious reasons his statement is far from popular. A modern equivalent might be the suggestion made to a congregation that it is actually the secular world which has pioneered concern about many of the agonies in today's society, the church very often limping up rather late in the process with offers to help. Suppose the preacher were to say that the action of those forces we think of as secular was motivated by that same Holy Spirit which the church is sometimes tempted to think of as its own possession! The device Jesus is using is something like that. The point is that not until he does this is there reaction.

> *When they heard this, all in the synagogue were filled with wrath*

Only now has something been heard. Isaiah's words were just as challenging and just as salutary, if not actually revolutionary; but because they are scripture they are not heard in such a way as to provoke response. Applying them in a contemporary way is what makes the difference. Then there really is a response with a vengeance!

> *They rose up and put him out of the city*

So often this is the reaction to a searing application of scripture. At first, people reject or dismiss the speaker in some way. He or she is young and hotheaded. He or she just doesn't understand the complexities of public affairs and public policy. This or that is not the proper agenda of the church. At worst, there can be charges of subversive intentions or Marxist leanings. Only after all this has been worked through is there some chance of dealing with the issues in a reasonable way.

To look at this episode in Nazareth is to look at a perfectly familiar pattern which takes place in contemporary Christianity when the task of facing unpleasant yet very real issues is attempted.

Psalm

Once again we see a pattern very often present in the psalms. The run of the verses presents a sequence of vivid images about God. They are almost quick videos of the nature of God. In rapid succession in these six verses we see God as a place of refuge, as deliverer, as the One who listens, as our stronghold, again as deliverer, as the basis for hope, as sustainer of life. Each one of the images is in itself capable of becoming food for reflection.

Fifth Sunday after Epiphany, Proper 5

Isaiah 6.1–8(9–13)
1 Corinthians 15.1–11
Luke 5.1–11
Psalm 138

Theme In each of the scriptures we see a person or certain people made to realize the power and the presence of God in and for their lives. In his temple vision Isaiah is overcome by the majesty of God yet is also enabled to respond to its call (Isaiah). Paul decides to remind his listeners of what constitutes the heart of the Christian good news (Corinthians). By a simple action at the lake Our Lord consolidates the call already given to the disciples (Luke).

First Reading *In the year that King Uzziah died I saw the Lord*

This vision of the prophet is one of the greatest passages of sacred scripture. I will give most space to this scripture this Sunday. It is particularly significant for this generation because it expresses the situation in which contemporary humanity finds itself. It expresses the feelings, fears, insecurities, and hopes of many today. Isaiah lives in the time of the king's death. What is literally true for him is true at many other levels for us. If "the king" means all those elements of society which hold authority, then this is an age of the deaths of "kings." Assumptions, traditions, structures, institutions are all dying, at least they are in flux. The result is an age of extreme anxiety and distrust of the future; in a word, an apocalyptic age.

I saw the Lord

Yet it is precisely in such a turmoiled age of history that many people have a sense of rediscovered spirituality. They see the Lord in a new way, with new intensity and a renewed sense of being called to serve him in some way. Much of that is happening all around us. Whether in the lives of ordinary unknown people or of very well-known figures, we are seeing the rediscovery of the significance of faith.

Sitting upon a throne, high and lifted up

Contemporary spirituality is a heightened spirituality in many senses. First of all, it is increased in intensity. By and large, bland religious faith has disappeared. If faith is present at all, it tends to be seriously held. There is something in the air that is letting us know that the stakes have got higher where faith is concerned. Modern faith is also heightened by the sense of mystery that today's world engenders in us. Within the worship life of faith, there is an awakening of our liturgical senses. The action and images and symbols of the faith are being renewed by the recovery of rich associations. The sacramental acts are becoming richer experiences for many. The lovely and powerful mysteriousness of Baptism and Eucharist is speaking to many to whom worship had become familiar and perhaps even mechanical.

[God's] train filled the temple . . . the whole earth is full of his glory

The glory of God fills both the temple and the world. First, the division between temple and world is taken away. The mystery of God is today no longer imprisoned in the religious. The issues of our time are so vast that there is a sense of mystery about almost any aspect of the human scene. The ways in which we are born or not born, in which we die or do not die, the interrelating of our bodies, minds, and spirits, the nature of health as wholeness, the possible place for us in outer space — all such things are now the arena of "God-sized" or "soul-sized" questions. The song of the seraphims is in many ways increasingly our human song as we are forced into an acknowledgement of the awesomeness of contemporary existence.

The seraphim . . . flew

The seraphim in reality were fixed wooden figures in the temple of that time. In his vision Isaiah saw them flying. There is a truth there for us. Everything which we have thought of as fixed and unchanging is now being changed. Nothing any more is static or predictable for us. Everything is undergoing re-forming before our eyes.

The foundations of the thresholds shook

That is very true of us. The foundations of our thinking, of our society, our civilization, of the way we think about our humanity, of the way we think about God are all being shaken.

The house was filled with smoke

Contemporary existence is engulfed in smoke in two senses. Smoke can mean danger, confusion, threat, even death. All these realities are around us. But smoke can also mean incense, the promise of the presence of the divine even in our darkness and confusion and danger. In which sense are we prepared to see the reality around us?

Woe is me! For I am lost

Before the human prospect today many feel a sense of great inadequacy. They feel they cannot respond; sometimes they even find it difficult to function. There is much fear and depression and hopelessness, much covering up these things by such pointless activities as consumerism. The bumper sticker "Born to Shop" or "When the going gets tough the tough go shopping" is actually a sad summary of much modern nihilism.

A different kind of inadequacy, a much more creative one, is the inadequacy we feel before the call of God. Isaiah feels this. He knows he is called, but he feels he is not worthy of that call. We feel that. We feel we have nothing to offer. But Isaiah expresses even more than this. What he says next is the expression of a very late twentieth-century experience.

I dwell in the midst of a people of unclean lips

Isaiah feels not only that he is personally unworthy but that the society he lives in is unworthy. He has lost faith in its institutions and its structures. That is true of millions of people today. There is a great deal of political and social cynicism abroad, a loss of trust in the body politic.

For my eyes have seen the King, the Lord of hosts

It is easy to miss the significance of this part of the verse. The reason that Isaiah feels a sense of unworthiness both about himself and his society is that he has seen a vision of the glory and beauty and quality of God. These days many men and women have had their faith in the future renewed by a vision of what their own society can be, what international relations can be, and how different the distribution of the world's resources can be, if we are prepared to pursue peace and justice. It is true that this can come to many as a secular vision, a humanist commitment. To say that is not to denigrate such a vision. This same vision can be ours in Christian terms. It exists in the hearts and minds of many Christians and is the spur for their commitment and their work and very often their great sacrifices.

A burning coal . . . from the altar. And he touched my mouth

Isaiah's paralysing sense of inadequacy is met by an offer of grace. All through the Bible God does this. God will call. The human recipient of the call will decline. He or she will be fearful or feel unworthy. God does not retreat from the call. God offers some means of grace and then reiterates the call until there is acceptance. It is for us to ask what God's burning coal is for us! What offers us grace? Some gift we have never used within ourselves? The help of another person we have never accepted? The grace hidden in our religion which we have never paid much attention to? What has always been in our lives that we have never really allowed ourselves to be deeply touched by?

Your guilt is taken away . . . your sin forgiven

Our guilt paralyses us. This gives us a sense of inadequacy. We feel unworthy. But the really great news of the Bible, said again and again in case we do not hear it the first time (which we very rarely do), is that God has already taken away our guilt and forgiven us! God has forgiven us long before we have got around to forgiving ourselves! This realization is what enables Isaiah to hear the repeated call of God and allows him to say his resounding yes. Will this be true for us? To make it come true is the whole point of our spiritual journeying and wrestling.

> *Go, and say to these people: 'Hear and hear, but do not understand'*

Isaiah receives a chilling responsibility. It is made very obvious that what he has said yes to is by no means a simple task. Saying yes to God can be a salutary experience. Having the grace of God does not mean that some terrible obstacles to our succeeding will be wafted away by some magic.

> *How long, O Lord?*

A very human question which we have all asked at some time or other. We have asked how long a certain situation will go on. We have asked how long we can stand things as they are, how long we can remain faithful to whatever commitments we may have made, how long we can keep from breaking.

> *Until cities lie waste without inhabitant, and houses without men, and the land is utterly desolate*

Notice how grimly contemporary these images are. These are the images of a postnuclear landscape. One is not being merely melodramatic. While it is, thank God, not true that God has asked us to be faithful in such a landscape, nevertheless it exists in the modern psyche.

Many feel it looming over their lives and the lives of their children. To many it seems inevitable. We all live and work and serve in a nuclear-threatened consciousness. This is where God asks us to be faithful and hopeful.

> *An oak, whose stump remains standing when it is felled*

One of the great examples of the unconquerable nature of biblical hope. As we walk through a world that sometimes seems like a wilderness and even like a desert to us, we are to look out for anything that can be seen as hope for the future. For Isaiah this is symbolized by the pathetic stump of a felled tree. But that stump is actually the source of new life in that desert. So our vocation in the sometimes wilderness and desert of contemporary existence is to be men and women who are ready to grasp all possibilities for good and for grace and for God, to work with them and to use them to build the future God wills.

Second Reading   *I would remind you . . . in what terms I preached to you the gospel*

As Paul sets out to do this for his people in Corinth we might agree that it is a good thing for each one of us to do. It means setting aside certain occasions to think seriously of what the gospel really means for us in our own life. It means asking at thoughtful times, What is it that I truly believe? It may mean deciding to take a kind of refresher course in our faith, perhaps through a program in our parish or in a local community college's religion department, or in a nearby seminary which may have an outreach program. We need to be reminded of the terms in which we have heard the gospel preached to us.

The gospel, which you received

It is good sometimes to remember how we came to be a human being of faith. How did the church come to mean to us what it does mean? Who was the person to whom we owe whatever faith we possess? Was that some one person more than others? Have we ever really said "thank you" for that? How did we get this great gift?

The gospel . . . in which you stand

To what extent is the gospel the ground I stand on? To what degree is it the basis for my thinking and my deciding? In what sense is it the solid rock I can stand on in a heaving world? That does not mean that nothing in my faith or my church must ever change. Life is change.

The gospel . . . by which you are saved

It is easy to take for granted the great traditional language of the faith. Jesus is my Saviour. What does that mean when the chips of life are down? What does faith in my Lord save me from? In what sense does it save me from myself and what I would otherwise be? Sometimes, when I look at how Jesus wrestled triumphantly with his own humanity, I am given the grace to wrestle with my own. He then saves me from being overcome by my own humanity and its weaknesses.

If you hold it fast

The gospel is not merely received and then taken for granted in one's life. It has to be held on to. There are times when life and its events may try to take the gospel from us. Pain can do that, so can sorrow. Temptations of one kind or another can also steal our faith from us. There are many reasons why we have to intentionally keep our hold on the gospel once given to us.

(There is much more in this very rich passage but we must also look at the third scripture.)

Third Reading   *[Jesus] sat down and taught the people from the boat*

Jesus came into Peter's workaday world and uses the things of Peter's job to do the Lord's work. That is exactly true of us if we are prepared to let it be so. Christ is not content to be isolated to the "church" part of our existence. Our commitment there, necessary and good though it be, is only a symbol of the other areas of life we need to commit to Our Lord.

Put out into the deep

There are moments when Our Lord wants us to go further, to explore areas of ourselves where we have perhaps never risked going "deep," maybe because we didn't know such an area existed, or perhaps we have known only too well that it exists and are fearful of what we will find.

Master, we toiled all night and took nothing

It may be an area of our lives which we have given up on. It has produced only frustration and disappointment.

They enclosed a great shoal of fish

Under the probings of Our Lord's grace we decide to try that area again, and to our astonishment we discover far more than we expected.

> *They beckoned to their partners in the other boat to come and help them*

In fact, we discover so much that we cannot handle on our own. It may force us to reach out for new relationships and perhaps enter into wider community. community.

Psalm

A beautiful and heartfelt expression of gratitude to God. Notice how the psalmist's thoughts of God vary from the very personal to the wide horizons of the nations. God is the God of kings and nations but also, to use Evelyn Underhill's lovely phrase, he comes "across the low lintel of the human heart."

Sixth Sunday after Epiphany, Proper 6

Jeremiah 17.5–10
1 Corinthians 15.12–20
Luke 6.17–26
Psalm 1

Theme In all three scriptures and the psalm a set of opposites is put before us. In each we must choose and there is little middle ground. Jeremiah warns us against trusting in our own selves and our own judgement to the exclusion of God (Jeremiah). Paul puts before us the resurrection claim of the faith and insists on its centrality for a Christian (Corinthians). Our Lord puts before us the standards of his rule and kingdom. To say that they challenge our standards is an understatement (Luke).

First Reading *Cursed is the man who trusts in man . . . whose heart turns away from the Lord*

At first sight this is one of those passages which gives an excuse for those who wish to fulminate against the intrinsic evil of human nature. If we read the whole verse rather than merely the first half, we become aware that it is not dismissing human nature as something cursed. It is important to point this out because there is much in today's religious atmosphere which is only too ready to rail against the evil in human nature. We are in an ambivalent mood about ourselves. In the advertising world we use seductive slogans like "Give yourself the credit you deserve." At the same time we dislike much of what our human activities have accomplished. We realize that we have done immense damage to the earth and that we are capable, unless we choose otherwise, of actually destroying it as a liveable habitat. Our pornography is a strong hint that we do not like ourselves overmuch.

> *Whose heart turns away from the Lord*

This phrase is important. It is not being human that makes us evil. We only become evil when our self-trust and self-centredness turn us away from God. In the Genesis story Adam and Eve are not intrinsically fallen creatures. They only become so when they place their own will in opposition to divine will.

> *Like a shrub in the desert . . . in the parched places . . . in an uninhabited salt land*

If the self becomes the hub of one's existence, its wants and plans and ambitions and power diminish. Eventually the essential flow of life dries up. It dries up because the self as a source of life is limited. There are great resources in the self. That is quite obvious. After all, the self in a human being is the creation of God, no matter how we appropriate it and deny God access to it. But left to itself, its flow of creativity, its ability to love, its tendency to dream dreams, its capacity for such things as generosity and self-sacrifice — all eventually dry up. Here I am using the same images as the prophet does. The self becomes a desert where the streams of various kinds of life dry up.

> *Blessed is the man who trusts in the Lord*

(There is a beautiful subtlety in the second part of this verse which we will look at in a moment.) Jeremiah is proclaiming the experience of millions of men and women. To trust in a source of grace and life beyond ourselves, particularly if that source is the creating and grace-giving God, is to discover a never-ending resource for our living.

> *The man . . . whose trust is the Lord*

I think more is meant here than just a poetic echo of the first phrase. This speaks of an even deeper level of trust which some have reached. If the Lord has become my trust, then my self and my will have been absorbed into the will of God. We have become one. Perhaps only a great and deep saintliness can reach this state. We have a slight intimation of it in our human relationships. We will meet someone who comes to mean much, even everything, to us. We walk with them, share with them, love them. Years pass by and we discover that each has so deeply entered the existence of the other that each can say, "You have become my love." There are those for whom God has become utterly their trust.

> *He is like a tree planted by water, that sends out its roots by the stream*

How do I become the kind of man or woman who, having realized that God is the ultimate source of grace for my life, intentionally directs my energies towards that source, not merely waiting for it to come to me. What might sending out "roots by the stream" mean? It could mean developing my prayer life, being consistent in worship, realizing the power of the sacraments for my life, becoming aware of Scripture as a source for my thinking and reflection.

> *Does not fear when heat comes . . . the year of the drought*

If I do these things, I am at least armed for the times when pressure and challenge enter my life, when there can be pain or suffering of various kinds. Times of "heat" can also mean those occasions when my spirit dries up, when God seems absent, life pointless, the prospect dark. Such times can be within my soul "the year of the drought," which we have all known.

> *Not anxious in the year of drought, for it does not cease to bear fruit*

Notice that the man or woman "whose trust is the Lord," who is "a tree planted by water," does not thereby escape the year of drought. None of us escapes such times. The question is not how we can escape that experience by taking various religious steps to prevent it. There are no such steps. All of us must experience that kind of drought. The question is whether we have the resources within us from God to continue to function creatively as spiritual beings during such times.

> *The heart is deceitful above all things, and desperately corrupt*

An important warning. We are not only capable of deceiving others but also we are just as capable of deceiving ourselves!

> *I the Lord search the mind and try the heart*

Let us be aware of something very important here. God will not force a way into our hearts and minds. I am a free being and must choose to open heart and mind to God. Only if I submit to the entering of God into heart and mind, will the dark places of my being be illuminated and my motives directed and cleansed.

Second Reading   *How can some of you say that there is no resurrection of the dead?*

Sometimes we think that modern doubts about the resurrection of Our Lord are an aspect of the agony of contemporary faith, that up to now Christians found the resurrection faith somehow easy and natural. Nothing could be further from the truth. This passage shows us that, even in the opening generation of Christianity, the minds of men and women had to wrestle with this tremendous claim.

> *If Christ has not been raised, then our preaching . . . and your faith is in vain*

Paul is adamant that the heart of Christian faith is the resurrection. We must be aware that Paul is not in the least concerned to pile up evidence about an empty tomb. That may seem at first sight contradictory. It is not. For Paul, the blinding truth (in his case quite literally blinding) is that God has raised Jesus Christ. Christ has gone beyond the mere humanity he shared with us. He has taken that humanity and lifted it with him to a higher level of being. For Paul this is the resurrection. The great changing factor for Paul was that the risen Christ appeared to him from this higher level of being, capturing his heart and his life.

> *If Christ has not been raised . . . you are still in your sins*

When we say that Christ is risen, we are also saying something immensely hopeful and affirming about our own humanity. We are saying that Our Lord, having assumed our humanity (i.e., coming "down" to us), has in his resurrection raised up our humanity to the higher level of being he himself has attained. To try to put this great mystery very simply. . . if as a Christian I have committed myself to Jesus Christ as Lord, then, in spite of all the shortcomings of my personal humanity, that same humanity has been glorified by Our Lord's living it out. Moreover, it has been further glorified by his taking it "up" into the light and presence of God. In this way my hope is not contained only by this life. My bridge to a higher level of being is my Lord, who has himself crossed that bridge to me and returned across it again, bearing my human nature with him.

Third Reading *He came down with them and stood on a level place*

It seems as if Luke, in this very long verse, is dwelling on the scene, storing it up in his memory. I find myself asking why. Is it because it vividly portrays our belief that in Christ God came "down" among us, that God in Christ emptied himself and, as Paul says, "made himself of no reputation." In saying that Jesus "came down with them and stood on a level place," Luke is giving us an image of the loving God who in Jesus Christ stands on a level with our humanity, looking at us face to face, divine power and glory willingly laid aside. Notice Luke's description of the scene. . . .

> *Great crowd of disciples . . . multitude of people . . . who came to hear him and to be healed*

Nothing has really changed. We live in a world of great longing for that which will guide and heal all that needs guidance and healing in human experience. That longing has not one whit abated down the centuries of the human condition.

> *Those who were troubled with unclean spirits were cured*

Unclean spirits are not a long-ago phenomenon. Our time is only too well aware of them. We may use different language, but what we speak of is the same reality. The end of our century is rife with the spirits of fear, cynicism, mutual mistrust, dread of our own achievements, self-hatred of what we know we are capable of doing and being — to make only a short list of the spirits of our time.

> *Power came forth from him*

It does today and will for ever! That may seem a very obvious thing to say, but there are many obvious things we are failing to say these days because we feel they can be taken for granted among Christians. They cannot be taken for granted! It is desperately important that Our Lord be seen as a living contemporary reality and not merely as an admirable memory! To know Jesus Christ as Lord in our time is to possess a source of grace and energy and power.

Blessed are you poor . . . you that hunger . . . you that weep . . . when men hate you

Perhaps nowhere does Our Lord show his power more than in his readiness to challenge utterly the standards we take totally for granted in our world. Jesus proclaims a kind of alternate moral universe where all values are reversed and a terrifying reality is disclosed to us. Our affluence is shown essentially to be poverty, while what seems poverty to us is shown to be incredibly rich. One example of this is the consistency of the reports of those who return from areas of the world where the conditions of life are in our terms ghastly. As they speak of their experience, we invariably hear of the prodigal generosity of their hosts even if there is almost nothing available to share. share.

Woe to you that are rich . . . that are full now . . . that laugh now

Our Lord, pointing to wherever there is affluence, seeming high achievement, comfort, success, self-satisfaction, demands that we be accountable for what we have. Our Lord is not saying that affluence and comfort and success are of themselves evil. He demands that there be sharing, and that there be absolute accountability for the way we use and distribute such possessions. In fact, the Bible would say that we are not to think of such things as possessions, but as gifts received and, therefore, calling for responsible use.

Psalm

As we read the images of this psalm they echo those of the Jeremiah passage. Godlessness is portrayed in terms of dryness, godliness in terms of streams. We hear this again in verses 3 and 4 of the psalm. There is another voice in Christian spirituality for whom the presence and absence of God is voiced in such images. It is the voice of Hildegard of Bingen, forgotten for centuries but now sounding again in the life of the church. Her volume in *Classics of Western Spirituality* is worth reading. The images are particularly well and simply expressed in the prayer after the psalm (page 705, *BAS*).

First Sunday in Lent

Deuteronomy 26.1-11
Romans 10.8b-13
Luke 4.1-13
Psalm 91.9-16

Theme The ultimacy of God. We first hear the people of God being told in no uncertain terms that all they have and all they are is the gift of God. They owe God everything! (Deuteronomy). We hear Paul telling his readers that Jesus as risen Lord is an ultimate object of faith in a Christian's life (Romans). We then read in the temptations of Our Lord his reiterated statement that God is the value and the standard over all other motivations for our decisions and actions (Luke).

First Reading *The land which the Lord your God gives you for an inheritance*

The land itself is a gift. We do not own it. Our culture, which puts so much store in the ownership of land, has never really easily heard this kind of scripture. Other voices have said it to us, those of native spirituality. For the most part we traded on the incapacity of Indian peoples to understand land as something to be owned. In many ways we betrayed them. Sometimes we expressed contempt for their naiveté. We went on to build a culture which too easily has seen land as something to be used as we wished, exploited if necessary. Only now, in the late years of the century, are we realizing the high cost of some of our decisions and actions. The Bible is uncompromising on this issue; everything we possess is the gift of God. We are not possessors but the stewards of creation and its bounty.

> *God gives [it to] you for an inheritance*

The fact that we have received creation as an inheritance implies that we are responsible for how we hand it on to generations after us.

> *God gives you . . . [you] have taken possession of it*

Notice the co-operation between God and humanity. The fact that we have taken possession does not lessen the fact that what we possess is a gift. We may have ownership but it is a delegated ownership. Again the word to describe us in this situation is *steward*. It is becoming a most important word as our humanity develops the capacity to do infinite harm to the gift of God.

> *You shall take some of the first of all the fruit of the ground*

Notice that we are to take the first fruits. Our giving to God is not to be an afterthought, a grudging last minute throwaway in the direction of a pestering God. Over and over in this great passage the implication is that all we possess is the gift of God. We owe everything to God!

> *You shall go to the place where the Lord your God will choose, to make his name dwell there*

A beautiful thought, that there are places where God calls us to make God's name dwell there. Where have you and I gone that we have made God's name to dwell there, by something we said or did, some witness we made, some commitment, some act of love or statement of faith?

> *You shall make response before the Lord your God*

And what is that response here in this scripture? It is to tell the story of one's life — the wanderings, the experiences of joy and sorrow, the imprisonment and release, the passage through wilderness, the attaining of a new land. The reason why these verses are significant for every reader is that each one of us has made and is making such a journey.

> *A wandering Aramean was my father*

Wandering.... When was I in a wandering stage of my life? When did I search about for a direction? Teen years? Different stages of professional career? Marriage?

> *Went down into Egypt . . . few in number . . . there he became a nation*

Where and in what stages and for what reasons have I had to spend some time feeling weak and vulnerable, having to grow and prove myself resilient and capable of surviving? How has that formed me? Can I now see the hand of God in my life in that testing time?

> *Hard bondage*

Have I experienced times of real injustice? Millions have and are living with this sense of being "in Egypt." Do I really hear them when they try to convey to me their hurt and anger and pain? Or do I dismiss them as radicals and brand their spirituality as subversive liberation theology? Do I understand when they read into such scriptures as this their own story?

> *The Lord brought us out of Egypt*

Do I ever count what God has done for me? Do I take my blessings for granted as my due and my right? What has God brought me out of? Have my "Egypts" been depressions, crises, the consequences of wrong thinking and deciding, unhappy relationships, a sense of imprisonment in my job? There are many Egypts in human experience. The scripture says that God's bringing us out of them can be "with terror." Winning our freedom from the various prisons in which life has put us can be costly.

> *A land flowing with milk and honey*

What elements of "milk and honey" have I been given? What blessings are mine? What destinations have I managed to arrive at, even though I have to travel further?

> *Now I bring the first of the fruit of the ground, which thou, O Lord, has given me*

Having thought about this magnificent passage of scripture in this way, are we now ready to think again about our expressions of thanksgiving to God? How do we feel about the response we make to God? How do we feel about those gifts we bring to "set down" before God?

Second Reading *The word is near you, on your lips and in your heart*

This is one of those great statements in scripture which can speak on many levels of meaning. The word is near us. That has to be true of our approach to scripture. When we read the Bible, we need to realize that the reading is not merely for remembering things which once happened. The substance of the passage is not far away in time and, for us in North America, in distance. It is not about long-ago people and far-away events. It is about us; it will always be about those who read it. It will speak to their time and probe their hearts. The Bible is a "now" book. It is that quality which continually makes it a word from God to us. It is in every sense near us.

On your lips and in your heart

Obviously it must be both. To have the word of God perpetually on one's lips without it being in the heart is obviously hypocritical. But having said that, there is something to reflect on in both images of lips and heart. There is a kind of fervent Christian faith today which certainly does have the Bible on its lips. Texts can be quoted for every situation. Sometimes, however, we can get the impression that the Bible is not altogether in that person's heart. Our Lord's love and deep respect for persons is missing. One feels oneself to be the target of texts shot like ammunition against a foe. One does not feel loved so much as captive. On the other hand, there are people who do carry the word of God in their heart, to whom the Christian faith is significant, for whom worship is an integral part of life, for whom the Lord Jesus Christ is present in word and sacrament and in other people, but who never by a single word speak any witness to what all this means to them for their daily life! That totally silent Christianity is very much part of most mainline Christian life. However, from time to time there are moments which can be used to communicate tastefully and sensitively that the Christian faith is a significant resource for one's life. In that way Christian faith can be offered to another person who may be seeking for God.

> *If you confess with your lips that Jesus is Lord, and believe in your heart that God raised him from the dead, you will be saved*

Of course we will be, but the reason why many have difficulty responding to this great statement is that they have difficulty understanding what being saved might mean. Many people have consigned such language not only to a religious ghetto but to a certain part of that ghetto, certain traditions for which such language seems to have meaning. In one way we could answer the question, What does Jesus Christ save me from? by saying that Christ saves me from what I need to be saved from! And what is that? In one huge word it is *self*. Self that wishes to rule my life, insists on being its centre, and continually demands more attention and more power. We might ask another question, What does Jesus Christ save me for? The answer is that Christ saves me from self, not to crush the self and make me less who I am, but to purge and change that self so that I may be more the person God wills me to be. As C.S. Lewis once said, the difference between Satan and Our Lord is that, while Satan wants only to possess us until we disappear as persons, Our Lord wants to possess us only to give us back our selves, so that we can be even more who we are! Satan devours; Our Lord empowers!

First Sunday in Lent

Third Reading   *Jesus, full of the Holy Spirit, returned from the Jordan, and was led by the Spirit . . . in the wilderness*

The really important thing to note from this scripture is that the same Spirit which is present with Jesus in the excitement of his baptismal experience is also present with him in his experience of the wilderness. That immediately says something to us about our own experiences. It is very easy in life to feel the presence of God in times of achievement and celebration. It is also very easy to presume at other times — times of suffering, confusion, anxiety — that the Holy Spirit is absent from our lives. We think that if the Spirit were present we would not feel as we do. But we see in Our Lord's life that the Holy Spirit actually takes him into a period and into a place of wilderness. We also see that this happens for a purpose. The wilderness becomes the place where Our Lord wrestles with options for the future and decides his course of action.

It might be worthwhile to use a moment of silence in a homily such as this. Each one might think back to a time in life which felt like a wilderness time when we were going through it, but which we now realize was a time of forming and planning and seeing some next steps. If we could come to see that there have been times when the Spirit of God took us into a wilderness period for a purpose, it will be a great deal easier for us in future wilderness times to feel a presence with us.

The devil said . . . "Command this stone" . . . showed him all the kingdoms . . . set him on the pinnacle of the temple

If we look at the series of temptations, we see a certain pattern. All the temptations seek to draw Our Lord into the kind of action which puts self and its strengths and gifts first. Again, all the temptations are such as to use power in some form, to build empires of some kind. It is extremely important to realize that, on the surface and judging by the standards of the world in every age, not one of the temptations is other than reasonable practice!

The first option offered Jesus is what we might call the politics of bribery. Promises are made and initially fulfilled. A following is attracted by supplying a need. But the supplying of need becomes twisted in that the real motivation is not the fulfilling of need but the gaining of power. The second temptation we might call the politics of image. The would-be leader develops an image of wondrous abilities and powers. For him the world seems to work. He or she seems to have that longed-for thing we call control. He or she comes across as glamorous, larger than life. The third temptation is the politics of power. There are the "kingdoms of the world" for the taking. The only condition is that one must not be squeamish about it. After all, it is only reasonable that power has to be paid for in some way. Is the utter loss of integrity worth it? The loss of one's humanity?

To each of the temptations Jesus responds in the same way. Each response is slightly different in words but the same point is made. God is the ultimate standard and value and measure of thought and action. All other considerations, especially all quests for personal power, stand under the judgement of that ultimate. All human actions are judged in this way.

Psalm

Underneath the vivid exaggerations of the Eastern poet, a single truth is being expressed. The person whose total trust is founded upon God will not be betrayed by that same God. It might be very suitable this Sunday to sing Luther's great expression of this theme (*The Hymn Book*, No. 134).

Second Sunday in Lent

Genesis 15.1-12, 17-18
Philippians 3.17—4.1
Luke 13.31-35
Psalm 127

Theme There is a thread running through the scriptures which is about trusting and remaining firm. Abraham's basic insecurity makes it difficult for him to trust God (Genesis). In a world of widely differing values Paul exhorts his listeners to trust those values which are centred on Jesus as Lord (Philippians). Jesus upbraids the city of Jerusalem and its society for their inability to trust what he offered them (Luke).

First Reading

One way we might consider reading this passage is to see in Abraham the fears and the insecurities and the longing for guarantees that exist in all of us.

Fear not, Abram, I am your shield

In many ways we receive reassurance about life. We receive it early in life from those around us who love us. They may not express it in words but, if our relationships are healthy, they communicate somehow to us that life is essentially trustworthy. They tell us about that same God to the degree they can. By the very nature of life and relationships, we also cannot help picking up from our elders some of their deep-seated fears and wonderings about life. In a good relationship these should take second place to the positive messages we are given.

> *O Lord God, what wilt thou give me*

This passage illustrates the incredible courage and honesty of the Judaic tradition. Its heroes are never shown without their feet of clay. Their humanity is never avoided. Here is the great Abraham sounding like a small child bargaining with a parent. We often stand in Abraham's place in our attitude to life. There are moments when we enter the trap of expecting things to fall into our lap, when we succumb to the illusion that the world owes us a living, or when we expect things to come our way without any effort on our part. As we well know, great can be our resentment when our expectations are not fulfilled!

> *I continue childless . . . thou has given me no offspring*

Notice how quickly the first statement, which is one of mere fact, changes to the second, which is blaming God. It is very easy to slide from one to the other in our lives, to refuse to take responsibility for certain situations. This theme is really the basis of Scott Peck's bestselling book in recent years *The Road Less Travelled.*

> *[The Lord] brought him outside and said, "Look toward heaven, and number the stars"*

Sometimes in our fears and insecurities, in our self-questionings and doubts, in our times of refusing to be responsible for our lives, God takes us "outside," outside of our stunted selves, and forces us to look at life in a bigger way. He makes us "count the stars." When did I last go outside and count the stars? Sometimes a whole congregation needs to do that — to find their place in a larger people of God, to be reminded of their blessings and their responsibilities, to realize that the tensions and the questions they face are challenging the whole church and the whole of humanity!

> *Number the stars, if you are able to number them*

Is there a hint of God's rebuke there? Is God referring to the fact that, if we are not careful, if we get wrapped up in our fears and insecurities and resentments, we can lose the capacity to "count the stars," to think and to see and to act in a bigger way?

> *So shall your descendants be*

God is saying to Abraham what God sometimes longs for us to hear. God is pointing out what this fearful, insecure individual can become. He or she can become much much bigger than he or she is. There is much more in us than we sometimes dare to suspect. That is what the images of this verse are saying.

> *He believed the Lord. . . . But he said, "O Lord God, how am I to know?"*

Again, notice the wonderfully honest humanity of this moment. Abraham is very like the rest of us. We are reassured, and for a while we are secure again. But then all the old fears come back like a flood. Maybe what we have been told is not really true. Maybe we have been gullible. Maybe there are possibilities of threat and danger we have not even suspected. Thus sound the "three o'clock in the morning" voices of our fearful souls. We cry out with Abraham in a hundred ways, "But how am I to know?"

> *A deep sleep fell on Abram . . . a dread and great darkness fell upon him*

In how many of the great writings of human experience does this moment come? There is a time in every human life when one must enter into a dark place and wrestle with one's private demons. To emerge from that place one must wrest some element of even temporary victory. The Bible is far too honest to pretend that there can be permanent victories which keep us preserved from the necessity to struggle again at some future time. Abraham in his dark dream, Moses on the slopes of Sinai, Elijah in his cave on Horeb, Jesus in his wilderness, Paul blind in the street called Straight — all of them know about the dark place where we must do our wrestling. And our knowing such stories gives us a host of companions when we must ourselves dream dark dreams, or enter a dark place of fear or anxiety or suffering or bereavement. The knowledge that they were graced by God is at least promise to us that we may expect the same grace.

Second Reading *Mark those who so live as you have an example in us*

Paul is speaking about the role models we choose in life. To a greater or lesser extent we all have role models, particularly when we are young. Billion-dollar industries today depend on giving a new generation role models, whether the romantically melancholic faces which inhabit the world of Ralph Lauren, or the magnified voices of the latest singing group. Adult society has its role models.

As I write, for almost eight years an elderly man named Ronald Reagan, in spite of many flaws, has embodied authority and imagination and integrity for millions of Americans. What Paul is saying is perfectly true. We will always seek models to imitate, lifestyles to copy. If this is so, then it is important what choices we make.

> *Many . . . live as enemies of the cross of Christ*

If the cross is the symbol of sacrifice, then millions today live as enemies of all that the cross symbolizes. For the motivation around which much of Western society moves is that of consumerism, the opposite of sacrifice. Our society certainly believes that it is more blessed to receive than to give.

> *Their end is destruction, their god is the belly, and they glory in their shame, with minds set on earthly things*

Paul is speaking in the context of a society which in the twilight of its faith system had become grossly materialistic, rapacious, and decadent. Very few, if any, of the excesses of our time were unknown to Paul's world. He would see much in common if he could travel in our cities. A yawning gulf between affluence and poverty, an obsessive relationship with sexuality, a prodigal use of resources, an inner emptiness of faith and meaning and hope.

It is very easy to twist this passage into a diatribe against a full living of life. Paul is not being life denying here. In fact, he is being life affirming. He is demanding a quality of life that is other than destructive and self-defeating. Paul is not saying that food does not have its pleasures, that sex is not a most precious and wonderful gift, that earthly things are not legitimately desirable. He is condemning a way of life that regards these things as all there is to live for. He is questioning the making of these things into ends rather than means, the means towards a rich and deep life which acknowledges God as its creator.

> *Our commonwealth is in heaven, and from it we await a Saviour*

Paul says two immensely important and creative things in those few words. He postulates a reality in and around and within everyday reality. This reality is more, not less, real than the space-time world we know. Paul calls it heaven. It is not a place in our sense of place, nor a far away future time. It merely *is*, and all creation exists within it, creation being only a segment of it. It is a realm where the rule of God is perfect and ultimate, not, as in space-time, partial and grudgingly allowed by human self-will.

The second thing Paul says is that a Christian looks to a future crowning and transformation of creation. Just as Jesus Christ lived human life in such a way as to show it capable of transformation, so God will effect such a transformation in the whole body of creation.

> *Therefore . . . stand firm thus in the Lord*

As a Christian, knowing your origin, your identity, and your destination is a help to standing firm when everything in your world is in change and turmoil. Even in a radically changing reality, if God be God, then there is a reference point, a reality by which to look for direction, by which to measure the events of one's time, their meaning, their value, their significance.

Third Reading *Some Pharisees came, and said to him, "Get away from here, for Herod wants to kill you"*

Is it not interesting that this warning is given by those very people whose image in the gospel is almost totally that of enemy of Our Lord? This supportive action may be a hint of something very fascinating which is taking place in modern biblical studies. As we learn more and more of the way in which the New Testament was written and of the times in which it was written, we are realizing that conditions in the life of the Christian communities deeply affected the way the writers remembered and expressed the past. For instance, by the time the Gospels other than Mark were written, relationships between the followers of Jesus and other Jews were deteriorating badly. Because the Pharisee party was by then giving leadership to a Judaism traumatized by the loss of the temple in Jerusalem (in A.D. 70), the Pharisees were seen as the enemies of the Christian movement. Some feel that this threatening image of the Pharisees was projected back into the lifetime of Our Lord. There is mounting evidence that the reality may not have been as one sided as we have been led to believe.

Having said this, it may be well to point out a problem with sections of the gospel such as this. It is easy to reflect on the passage in terms such as I have done above, but how can these verses be used for pastoral preaching? What have they got to say to our lives? What truths about Our Lord do they communicate?

[Jesus] said . . . Go and tell that fox

The reply is harsh and full of contempt. It shows a side of Our Lord very far from "gentle Jesus, meek and mild." It is one of those many glimpses we get in the gospel which tell us very clearly that Jesus was indeed a fully human person, feeling the challenges and pressures of life and relationships as we all do. Every single one of us lashes out at others from time to time. Sometimes we regret it, sometimes we feel it unavoidable. To do so does not separate us from Our Lord. He has felt all the gamut of feeling we experience. In our rages, our resentments, our temptations to hurt, he remains Our Lord and we remain his all-too-human servants.

> *It cannot be that a prophet should perish away from Jerusalem*

There is a strong hint of bitter sarcasm here. It is emphasized by Our Lord's very next sentence. He is all too aware that Jerusalem has been something of a killing ground for prophets, whether we mean actual killing or the many instances of rejection and outright dismissal. We see him wrestling with very strong feelings of which he is obviously not fully in charge. He is responding to a hostility surrounding him. Again he is with us and among us as totally human. There is a Christian stance which equates itself with the perpetual hiding of true feelings, the presenting of a bland, pleasant exterior, the avoiding at all costs of confrontation on the grounds that such behaviour is in some way not Christian. Nothing could be further from what we see in Our Lord's behaviour.

> *O Jerusalem . . . how often would I have gathered your children together*

There is immense and obvious frustration, disappointment, regret in this cry of Our Lord. It is the cry of someone who feels a certain amount of defeat. He has tried and he has partly failed. We all have known those moments in life when we are forced to recognize failure. We are not often pointed towards this reality in Our Lord's life, yet it is there. Thank God it is, because once again it allows us to identify our experience with his. To me, it is legitimate to use this passage as a series of glimpses into a very difficult hour of Our Lord's experience. To do so does not diminish his glory for us. It enhances his significance, because it shows him struggling to deal with the humanity that you and I must struggle with as we follow in his steps.

Psalm

Again basically about trusting God. Not only is it necessary for individuals, but it is also necessary in family life (the house). It is necessary in the whole body politic (the city). A life of frantic activism is not enough. Our family relationships should be a very high priority.

Third Sunday in Lent

Exodus 3.1–15
1 Corinthians 10.1–13
Luke 13.1–9
Psalm 103.1–13

Theme A recurring theme through all the scriptures is a demand on each one of us to take responsibility for the well-being of the community of which we are a member, be it family or congregation or society. Moses is called to play a major role in the formation of his people's future (Exodus). Paul tells a demoralized community that each member can become the means of its recovery (Corinthians). Our Lord sternly points out that we cannot lay at the door of certain individuals in a society the blame for shortcomings which may be throughout the whole society (Luke).

First Reading *Moses was keeping the flock of his father-in-law Jethro*

Once again the Bible shows us a familiar pattern. Moses experiences the presence of God when he is very much engaged in his day-to-day activities. It is a word to us to have an eye for such a possibility in our own lives. Are we prepared to assume that in the ongoing responsibilities of our lives we are sometimes invited into the presence of God?

He came to Horeb, the mountain of God

Again the same thought. In the pursuit of his work he comes to Horeb, the mountain of God. Are we prepared for the possibility that our work will sometimes bring us to sacred places? What for us might a sacred place be? Could it be a place or a situation where we have a chance of helping someone? A moment when we can take hold of a problem in our lives? An opportunity to forgive someone or to give them guidance?

The angel of the Lord appeared to him in a flame of fire out of the midst of a bush

The extraordinary appears within the ordinary. That is one of the great central themes of the Bible. God uses the ordinary to enter the world, even for the entry of God in human flesh into the world.

And Moses said, "I will turn aside and see"

To turn aside is essential. We live in the kind of culture which makes it very difficult to turn aside, to take time, to step off the treadmill and pause. An English poet asks, "What is this world, so full of care, If we've no time to stand and stare?" C.S. Lewis in his book *The Screwtape Letters* has an experienced devil give advice to a younger devil on the way to keep a seeker from discovering Christ. He advises that, every time the human being comes in contact with something that may draw him to Christ, the young devil should not struggle against the influencing factor. He should merely suggest that there are a couple of odds and ends of life to be looked after first — a phone call, a chore, a letter to be written, an errand to be run. By the time that is done the opportunity has passed.

It is only when Moses actually turns aside, when he has already made an initial response, that God calls to him. Moses has shown himself to be potentially a person who has time for the encounter with God in his life.

Moses said, "Here am I"

We might use this short phrase to emphasize something important even for our everyday encounters with others. To what extent are we persons who can be truly "here" with another person? Very often when we are with someone, we are only half or three quarters there. Part of us is elsewhere, thinking of the last thing or the next thing. The same is true of our worship. We have to some extent placed ourselves in the presence of God, yet sometimes we cannot say truly to God, "Here I am." Our state is better described by a small plaque on the desk of a friend of mine. It says, "You have my divided attention." Most often God has our divided attention, as indeed have other people.

Our truly being somewhere has to be an intentional presence. Moses takes off his shoes. Someone will say to us, "Won't you take your coat off?" It is a signal that you are truly welcome to stay a while. We all know the tiny signs by which a person betrays their true feelings about any human encounter. We can tell the quality of their commitment to the meeting, the quality of their being truly with us. But we sometimes forget that they can often tell the same of us by the tiny signals, conscious and unconscious, which we send!

"I am the God of your father". . . .
And Moses . . . was afraid to look at God

There are moments in life when we meet the majesty of God. Those are the moments when we

Third Sunday in Lent

encounter the beauty and terror of human existence. The moment may be one of ecstasy and joy or pain and suffering, of light or of darkness. In such moments we will encounter the essential mystery of life, and we will bow our heads before it, because we will experience that mingled terror and wonder we call awe or the fear of God.

> *The Lord said, "I have seen the affliction of my people . . . and I have come down to deliver them. . . . Come, I will send you"*

Even though God says, "I have come down," it is not a magic coming down of God. God is not a *deus ex machina*. God's coming down is linked with "Come I will send you." Anything God wishes to do in history, God finds a man or woman through whom to do it. In this case it is to be Moses. God is the supreme delegator. Karl Rahner once said that humanity is how God decided to appear in the world when God decided not to appear in the world as God. It is a magnificently succinct stating of a great and very ancient truth.

> *But Moses said to God, "Who am I that I should go to Pharaoh?"*

This is a classic biblical moment. God has issued the call and the human recipient at first steps back in fear from the challenge. We see it happen again and again. It is also a personal experience with many of us. God calls us to some task and our first inclination is to back away. It doesn't suit our gifts. It is not the right time to make the move. We won't be able to do it. If such and such were in the picture we could, but since it isn't, we can't. All those thoughts are perfectly familiar to most of us.

> *God said, "I will be with you"*

So very simple a series of words yet meaning so much, in fact meaning everything. But Moses, like most of us, is still very far from being persuaded.

> *If . . . they ask me, "What is [God's] name?" What shall I say to them?*

Moses thinks that, far from being suitable for missionary purposes, he is hardly aware of who God is! In our language, perhaps he feels he needs a great deal more theology! Almost all of us feel that. It is the great block to much lay witness in our time. In our mainline traditions many lay people think they won't know what to say when others ask them what the name of their God is. What does it mean to be asked the name of your God? It means being ready to express why we believe what we believe. Can we in some way name our God? Indeed we can, perhaps not with technical theological language; but that is not the language that attracts other men and women who are searching for faith. The simple, uncomplicated communicating to someone that the Christian faith meant a great deal to us as we went through some tough period — that is a powerful witness. That is very effectively telling the name of your God.

I AM WHO I AM

The deceptively simple words are flowing over with meaning. One thing they say is that God is very much NOW. God's name is not merely I WAS. It is not merely I WILL BE. God's name and nature is NOW, always and eternally NOW. When you and I sometimes succeed in getting across to someone what God means to us in our ongoing everyday experience, we are indeed saying that God's name is I AM. We are communicating the fact that God is not just a nice memory from our Sunday School days (I WAS), neither is God a pious hope for a far-away future or for our afterlife (I WILL BE). We are saying that for us God is NOW, God is I AM.

Second Reading *Our fathers were all under the cloud . . . all drank the same supernatural drink*

Paul is speaking to a Christian community in real trouble. They are in fact in a wilderness, largely of their own choosing and their own making. The community in Corinth is in a dreadful state of disunity, selfishness, snobbery, and a variety of immoralities. The first thing Paul wants to point out is that all this kind of thing has precedent in the history of God's people. There have been other wilderness journeys before this, particularly the Exodus. He quickly lists both the darkness and the terror of it all (the cloud and the sea), but he then tells of the resources they had for survival (the food and the drink). He even goes further. He tells how Moses took the elements of fear and terror and succeeded in transforming them into a baptismal experience of grace and recovery. Paul is implying that the Corinth community can do the same with its own problems.

They drank from the supernatural Rock . . . and the Rock was Christ

A sudden mystical insight of Paul's which he does not develop. It is an amazing thought he shares here. He is saying that in some mysterious way the grace of God's Holy Spirit, that same Spirit which a Christian sees embodied in Jesus Christ, was also the nourisher and the guide of God's earlier people in that long-ago journey. If we wish to use this passage in terms of personal experience, we could hear it saying to each one of us that the grace of Christ is present in our wilderness experiences.

Nevertheless . . . they were overthrown in the wilderness

There is always the possibility in our wilderness experiences that we too will be overthrown, that we will not be able to handle what life throws at us.

Do not be idolators as some of them were

Whenever the Bible speaks of idols and idolatry, we might think of it as saying that we must never make penultimate things ultimate. We must never give a supreme or ultimate value to something that is less than supreme. There is only one supreme reality — God. In a period of history that could be considered a wilderness period, many turn to different things as a substitute for God in their lives. It is not that these things are in themselves other than good. It's just that if we lift them to the highest level of value (i.e., if we make them our god), they let us down. When we do that, we are being in biblical terms an idolator. Our question then might be first on a personal level — What are our primary personal values to be on this wilderness journey God calls us to in the late twentieth century? The same question could be asked of the whole church.

We must not . . . grumble

It almost seems an anticlimax after the two other "must nots." Yet when you come to think of it, our attitude is all important. We and others are moving through a wilderness. Grumbling is a symptom of such things as anger, resentment, alienation — all things that tear apart a company on a common journey.

Let anyone who thinks that he stands take heed lest he fall

Paul is warning against the very common feeling in us all that "it cannot happen here to us." In this case what happened in Corinth can to some degree happen to any congregation. A congregation is at once a very strong and yet fragile thing. It only takes a few angry, resentful, alienated people to drain it of life. By the same token it takes only a small group of truly alive, joyful, committed people to affect the whole life of the community.

God is faithful . . . but with the temptation will also provide the way of escape

When a community is wrestling with strains and divisions, factions and disagreements, it is important to realize that, just as there exist those who create such things, so also there exist in the same community those whose gifts can be used for its health and recovery.

Third Reading *These Galileans . . . or those eighteen . . . do you think they were worse offenders than all the others who dwelt in Jerusalem?*

Jesus is exposing a tendency in society that is as prevalent now as it was in that day. Certain unhappy events take place. There may be a tragic accident, a brutal crime. The society is shocked, appalled, saddened, but it sees the event as essentially an aberration, something out of the norm. Perhaps blame is assigned either officially or unofficially. It is the work of this or that element, malcontents, radicals, criminals. Our Lord is asking us to consider the possibility that the event happened for a reason which involves the responsibility of the whole of society, or at least a great part of it. In the case of the tower of Siloam, instead of saying, "Maybe they deserved it anyway" (a phrase all too often used in any age to justify things a society does not wish to face) perhaps there might be some investigation as to why the tower fell in the first place. Perhaps we might find links between the weakness of the materials being used, the financial interests of those building it, and the graft of those granting licenses. Perhaps, instead of a few being blamed, many or all should do some repenting!

A fig tree planted in his vineyard

The tree is a vivid image of all aspects of God's creation — our personal lives, the communities and societies around us of which we are a part. All are created for one purpose — to bear fruit, to produce what God wills for us and for them. Our lives, the life of the church, the life of our country are accountable. That thought echoes Jesus' previous statements. He has been saying that we cannot place accountability on others without at least examining the possibility that in some way our responsibility is involved. The image of the tree extends that thought. Much patience will be shown us, much forgiveness will be accorded the various devices we use to evade responsibility and the demand of God for "good fruit" from our lives. Nevertheless, God demands accountability of each one of us.

Psalm

A song extolling the mercy and compassion of God, as its refrain says. Notice the typical biblical inclusion of the demand from God that there be judgement made on all oppression in society. Notice also the statement, "He has not dealt with us after our sins." It echoes Our Lord's statement in the gospel that we should not link untoward events as necessarily punishment for sin. Pastoral experience makes us realize the frequency with which people think this way, thereby unnecessarily punishing either themselves or others.

Fourth Sunday in Lent

Joshua 5.9–12
2 Corinthians 5.16–21
Luke 15.1–3, 11–32
Psalm 34.1–8

Theme In all the scriptures there is a sense of arriving at key moments in life when it is important to realize who we are and where we are and what we must do. Israel is between the desert and their first conquest in the new land. They take time to make the transition by observing traditions (Joshua). Paul insists that there must be times of decision in a Christian's relationship with Christ, once we realize what Christ has done for us (Corinthians). Our Lord speaks of those moments in our lives when in self-realization we can turn flight into return, abandonment into discovery, a dying into a new quality of living (Luke).

First Reading *This day I have rolled away the reproach of Israel from you*

The circumstances of this opening sentence seem very far from our lives. Israel has now travelled through the wilderness. They have come out of the hills to the east of the Dead Sea, and they are preparing to take the city of Jericho, which shimmers tantalizingly in its green oasis not many miles away. This particular time is a kind of breathing space. It is interesting how Joshua decides to use it. In the verse immediately preceding this passage he gives orders that all males are to be circumcised. Why at this stage in the journey? Why not before? It would seem that Joshua wanted to signify in some way that they had now arrived at a kind of Rubicon. A stage had ended in their history, the wilderness stage, and they had survived. In fact, they had more than survived, they had emerged as a people with high morale and an eagerness to seize the future. Joshua wants to act out in some way the break they have now made between past and future. In words we might use, they need to get Egypt totally out of their system (to roll away the reproach of Egypt). Hence the decision to carry out the act of circumcision.

Perhaps it's worth nothing that this step of Joshua's meant a period of physical pain for his men. It meant having to spend time waiting for healing. It meant being weak and vulnerable, all the things nobody wishes to have to do.

> *They kept the Passover*

Again, they do something quite out of the normal for the tension-filled days of their wilderness existence. They act out the roles of family life. They observe tradition. They relax.

> *They ate of the produce of the land,*
> *unleavened cakes and parched grain*

This moment has vivid memories for the writer. Here is unfamiliar food. Why mention this at all? Because, just like the circumcision, it is another symbol of leaving a past behind. The desert diet is over; now they eat the food of the land they have found. They become part of it and it becomes part of them. They are identifying. The writer specifically speaks of the ending of manna as a source of food. Manna was the godsend of the desert which had enabled them to survive. Now it was over. The writer repeats that fact, singing his joy like the verse of a psalm. You can almost feel him relishing the very words, "ate of the fruit of the land of Canaan that year." They are home!

So how do we use the passage for homily? One possibility is to think of our liturgical journey in Lent. We have passed the half-way mark. We too are anticipating a very terrible battle. We are moving toward the trial and the passion of Our Lord. How do we prepare for that? We have seen Joshua deliberately make his people pause between the two stages of their journey. They move out of activity into passivity. They observe ancient and gentle things of Passover. Life relaxes its demands for a short while. Is this a time in Lent to deliberately pause, perhaps to take a quiet time of some kind, on one's own or with others?

What might circumcision and Passover mean for us? The former can be anything which makes us aware of our own weaknesses and humanity, even our pain of many kinds. The latter helps us to become aware of the circles of relationship we live among. Why not use the former episode to begin to reflect about our bodies? Are we taking care of our bodies? What patterns of health or unhealth have we developed? Is tension growing? Does it have to? What intelligent limits should we consider acknowledging for our stage in life?

What might the symbol of Passover say to us? Are we giving time to relationships? Are we neglecting important ones? What ones are important? Do we have so many busy demanding acquaintances that we really have not time to develop real friendships? How about family? Do we talk to each other in any sustained way? Do we really know what is going on in each other's thoughts, or are we all taking each other for granted?

Yet another way to use the passage would be for reflection on the stage in life each of us is at. Is it a time to acknowledge that some things are naturally ending and others must begin? To deal with such questions we need, as Israel did, a time out, a quiet interval. Like Israel, do we need to take certain steps, to make certain decisions that mark out quite definitely this time of change for us? Are the battles ahead going to demand a different set of strengths from us than the battles behind us? To look at the passage this way might be very helpful to some.

Second Reading   *We once regarded Christ from a human point of view, we regard him thus no longer*

There are many ways in which we can regard Christ from a human point of view. We can relegate him to an illustrious place in history. We can compliment him on his ability to tell stories. We can admire his capacity for self-sacrifice. Many have done this in every century. A Christian also may grant Jesus Christ all these admirable qualities, but he or she cannot stop there. A Christian must decide whether this person is King for his or her life. A Christian cannot merely admire the stories. The question is, What do they mean for one's living? A Christian cannot merely think the cross rather courageous and noble. He or she must ask what this event calls one to become.

If anyone is in Christ, he is a new creation

To encounter Christ is to experience salient changes in oneself. One's self becomes occupied territory. It is not that one's self is obliterated. That is not Our Lord's way. Our self remains ours, but we find it joined by a companion self, Christ's self, if we can use that term. The way Paul trys to express the experience is to say that one's self and the "self" or Spirit of Christ, are reconciled. They, as it were, begin to sit down and talk together. There is something of that image in the Latin root of the word *reconcile*.

> *Gave us the ministry of reconciliation . . . entrusting to us the message of reconciliation. . . . We are the ambassadors for Christ*

A challenge to us. We don't merely have the luxury of experiencing an encounter with Jesus Christ. If he does indeed mean something significant in our lives, we are then faced with a question. If this reality in my life means so much, how do I communicate it to others? That seems to be a supremely difficult challenge in what we call mainline Christian traditions. There is a tremendous fear of being thought of as "religious" (heaven forbid!), as "holier than thou," as "having got religion," as a "Bible thumper." None of us wishes to be thought of in that way, but surely sometimes there are moments in our relationships when we can say that one of the resources in our own life is the Christian faith! The measure of how difficult that seems to have become today is an indication of the fearful degree to which our culture has locked Christian faith into the ghetto of the private and the personal.

Third Reading *The tax collectors and sinners were all drawing near to hear him*

Down the centuries shines that extraordinary paradox about Jesus of Nazareth. He embodies goodness, yet it never becomes a barrier to relationships. That goodness has not the chill which often enters into our human efforts at it! What was the secret?

> *This man receives sinners and eats with them*

Perhaps that was it. The ability to accept others totally for what they were. To be totally and effortlessly with them, so that they felt accepted and affirmed in a way that they had rarely experienced.

A man who had two sons

History will name this as the parable of the prodigal son. It is actually the parable of both sons. Among many other things this parable is about the complexities and subtleties of human development and human relationships. Jesus shows us ourselves while also speaking about our relationship with a loving God.

The younger said . . . Father, give me

It is a stage we all pass through. Some of us actually stay for ever in it. Its cry is always "give me." Our prayer life can stick at this stage and remain forever that simple, immature two-word prayer "Give me." It is also something else, this cry of the son. The self is now paramount in him. The universe circles around the self. It wants everything. It wants it now. Strictly speaking he should have said "the share that will one day fall to me." He wants the future now. All around us a multi-billion-dollar advertising industry uses this very device to make us respond. It suggests we can have anything now. In fact, it goes further sometimes. It suggests that it is our right to have everything now.

He divided his living between them

Notice the contrast. The father does not just give what is demanded. He divides the estate between them. This is easy to miss, and it is important. It tells us that whatever the older son is angry about later on cannot be that he has not got his share. The source of his anger must be elsewhere.

He squandered . . . he began to be in want . . . he joined to a citizen of that country

Vividly and swiftly we see the young man progress from innocence to a hard-won wisdom. It is a very contemporary pattern. We have a generation of millions who have never known anything but the inflated lifestyle of the last three decades. However, while some have achieved the heady heights of affluence, many more have begun recently to experience harsh economic realities unless there is care and hard work. Even the son being a swineherd gives us an image of a peculiarly modern phenomenon. Many people today, no matter what their qualifications, find that sometimes they must do just anything to get into the system.

When he came to himself

Those simple words describe a universal event in every life. In some it may be a particular moment when the scales drop from the eyes and we see ourselves as we really are. Sometimes we do not like what we see. Sometimes we live most of a lifetime before we come to ourselves, to use Jesus' vivid phrase. Occasionally it is another person who brings us to ourselves, sometimes lovingly and sometimes brutally. However we come to the moment, and whatever the quality of it, joyful or painful, it is the greatest gift we can receive. Now we have some chance of living with integrity and reality.

I will arise and go to my father

The prodigal sees his return in terms of a contrite criminal. He will confess. He will even suggest a penalty. We are all rather manipulative when we feel that survival is at stake!

But while he was yet at a distance, his father . . . ran

He still doesn't grasp the secret his father is trying to communicate to him. He asked for his share; the father divided all he had. He now comes prepared to confess and to plead, and he finds it is not necessary. The judge does not wait for the prisoner to approach. There is no judge, only a lover. Jesus is trying to teach us about our relationship to God and our relationships with one another, if we wish to have rich and deep relationships. The love of God is not a carefully calculated balance sheet of penalties and rewards. It does not exact a fee. Rather, it gives itself without calculation. The degree to which human love can emulate this truth is the degree to which it will reflect the divine love. In the parable, the father is trying to embody what he wishes his son to become. The great single truth he wishes to communicate is that life is about giving rather than getting.

> *The best robe . . . a ring . . . shoes . . . the fatted calf*

Notice that nothing is done by halves. One of the messages in this scripture is, if we are going to forgive, then let us forgive utterly, not grudgingly and by halves. One very human question we might wish to ask is whether the returning person deserves this. The answer comes ringing back to us that, of course, he does not! The point is that our deserts, thank God, are not the point! What has the Prayer Book sung most gloriously to us for centuries? It says that the nature of God is such as to give more than we can desire or deserve. That is what Jesus is teaching in the image of the father running towards the returning figure. And it is so easy for us not to realize that the figure is each one of us! God accepts, welcomes, affirms, and embraces who and what we are, imperfect and ashamed though we feel.

> *His elder son was in the field . . . he heard music and dancing. . . He asked . . . He was angry*

The vivid portrait of these two sons is so rich in meaning that one has to choose to reflect only on one facet of it all. There is a line in Tennyson which sadly has become one of the great clichés of the English language. It is sad because the content of the line is a very profound truth about life. Tennyson says that it is better to have loved and lost than never to have loved at all. That is at the centre of this story. The mysterious truth at the heart of life is that we have to lose certain things before we can really value them. Only after the younger son rejects love can he know it when he is brought face to face with it in his father. The elder, because he has never done so, cannot even recognize it when it shows itself to him in the father's obvious love.

There is an even deeper and more complex truth here. The son who did not deserve the father's love was able to receive it. The son who actually deserved it was not able to receive it. The older son is simply not capable of understanding the father's stance. Having never gone, he cannot come home. Having never lost, he cannot understand finding. Having never done any dying, he cannot understand language about being alive again. That is his tragedy. When we consider our own lives, we may come to see that by such paradox we too must fail in order to succeed, must lose love to find it, must do our times of dying so that we may taste resurrection.

Psalm

Just as Israel took time to celebrate their relationship with God by eating the Passover meal, just as the prodigal son uses a time of isolation and loneliness to do the same, so we need to take time to reflect on God's role in our lives. This is what the psalmist is doing. He deliberately calls to mind occasions when he was conscious of having received a strength beyond his own. To do this is a very simple yet powerful way to reaffirm our relationship with God.

Fifth Sunday in Lent

Isaiah 43.16–21
Philippians 3.8–14
John 12.1–8
Psalm 126

Theme In each of the scriptures there is anticipation of something totally new and quite extraordinary hidden in the immediate future. For Israel in exile the possibility of God's new action in history is their return from that exile. The stream of freedom will flow in the desert of exile (Isaiah). For Paul, his experience of Jesus Christ within himself is always promising new heights and new insights. (Philippians). For Our Lord, the action of Mary at an evening dinner is a symbol of the terrible reality that is soon to come, a terror that will make possible the unimaginable new reality of resurrection (John).

First Reading   *Thus says the Lord*

This is one of these Bible phrases so familiar that we can easily miss its significance. The assumptions behind the expression are radically different from those of our culture and time. The words assume that God is the Lord of life and events, that God has a purpose for all things, and that God in some way addresses our human experience.

Those assumptions are almost lost on our culture. To say "thus says the Lord" is to say that God is finally in charge. Millions today assume that humanity is in charge and, if we are not, that there is no other power. That very fact explains the considerable level of fear in today's world, because it is quite obvious that humanity does not always feel in charge!

Who makes a way in the sea

The presence of God is acknowledged in past history. The episode being referred to is of course the experience at the Red Sea.

Remember not the former things

The writer is not saying that these past events should be forgotten. To say so would be to deny much of the basis of Jewish religious observance. He is saying that, when we think about God, we should not remember only the past. If our thinking about God is in past terms then we very soon end up (as much of Western culture has done) with a past God! William Temple relates a moment in 1943 when taking a mission in Oxford University. As a quick test he asked a Bible study group to tell him the first response that came to their minds when he asked, "Does God know about atomic fission?" After a moment they laughed, because they realized that their instinctive response was to answer "No," and they realized that they were thinking, "Because it was after God's time!"

Behold, I am doing a new thing

God, implies the writer, must be thought of in terms of the formation of the future. If that is true, then somehow the hand of God is in contemporary events. That does not mean that God runs contemporary events like a puppet master operating a group of helplessly obedient figures. It means that the will and purpose of God is mingled with the will and purpose of God's free creatures, the human race. Human hopes, human will, human power struggles, human energy, human vision are all intertwined in the process of human events; and intertwined among them all is the will and purpose of the God who grants us creatures freedom to choose and freedom to decide and to act.

Do you not perceive it?

Today many do not. There are at least two tragic reasons why it is difficult for many worshipping Christians to think in terms of the participation of God in contemporary events. The first we have mentioned — the culturally created feeling that God "was" rather than "is." The second is even more subtle and difficult to challenge. For a number of centuries Western Christianity has been forced more and more into the private and personal areas of life. There God can be thought of in terms of my child's baptism or my father's illness. But the modern mind has great difficulty with the idea of God being a factor in the great flow of contemporary events, social and political. The irony is that millions of men and women in other cultures have no difficulty in thinking of God in these terms. The idea of God as the God of history is one of the great sources of energy behind the tides rolling in southern Africa and in Central and South America.

I will make a way in the wilderness and rivers in the desert

For those who believe that God is a contemporary creator, that God is involved in the processes of contemporary events, there is always the possibility that a wilderness period of history will lead to a new, liveable order for human life and human society. In the wilderness of events (which is a pretty fair description of the history we are living through today) there is a way through to the next chapter, and the co-author with us of that chapter is God. The image of rivers in the desert says to us that, in a period of history which feels barren, a time when such things as hope and joy and creativity seem to have dried up, there are still resources hidden in the desert, hidden in the situation, if we can but search and find them.

Second Reading *I count everything as loss because of the surpassing worth of knowing Christ Jesus as my lord*

Perhaps it is important to point out what Paul does *not* mean. He is not saying what some Christians choose to say when they discover the power of Jesus Christ in their lives. These Christians, in their new-found faith, will dismiss almost everything else in their experience as not of Christ. In extreme cases much of the culture surrounding them is dismissed as evil. Much contemporary writing, a great deal of art and music and drama, is judged to be of the world (used in an evil sense) rather than of God. It would seem as if the only way for God to be expressed in the world is in specifically Christian language and symbols! Paul is not saying this. The rest of Paul's life does not show this tendency in him. Often in his writings he is willing to use insights from the Greek civilization which formed him. All Paul is saying in this scripture is that everything else pales into insignificance compared to the paramount importance of Jesus Christ in his thinking.

For his sake I have suffered the loss of all things, and count them as refuse, in order that I may gain Christ

He had indeed lost a great deal for his Christian allegiance. It is obvious that the former Saul who became Paul could have wielded great influence in the circles of power of that time. He had the brilliance and the energy and the drive to do so. He chose otherwise. He chose to step from the centre of public life to the despised margin, even the very dangerous margin. The impetus which drove him to do that must have been terribly strong. It sprang from that devastating incident on the Damascus road when his world came apart and was put back together in a different way. That different way of understanding everything would mould him for the rest of his life.

> *Not having a righteousness of my own . . . but . . . the righteousness from God that depends on faith*

That was the essential difference between Saul and Paul, between his life before and after the Damascus road encounter. He saw that he was bound by ties even stronger than those of law. He was bound by love. He would obey, not because he had to obey but because he wanted to. He didn't have to give God some impossibly perfect Paul. God had accepted Paul as he was. Paul's task from then on was to respond to that devastating free acceptance God had shown. The same is true for every single one of us if we choose to recognize this massive truth at the heart of the Christian faith.

> *That I may know him and the power of his resurrection, and may share his sufferings*

For Paul the contrasting images of death and resurrection were always at the centre of his thought. Paul saw that Our Lord's death and resurrection were not only events to be recalled but were the essential pattern in Christian life, which had to be lived out again and again. Paul would say elsewhere that even in a daily sense we do some dying. His implication is that we also rise daily by Christ's grace.

> *Becoming like him in his death, that if possible I may attain the resurrection from the dead*

For Paul that did not mean something looked for at the end of his physical life. He certainly did have that hope, but it was also a hope for his ongoing daily life. Paul wished to live with a quality of death and resurrection about his whole life. Many times he tasted many kinds of dying, from physical suffering to deep despair. Many times he rose from those dyings and triumphed over the all-too-human feelings and weaknesses which he shared with the rest of us. But all this dying and rising Paul would have seen as the means of becoming like Christ and being open to the grace of Christ. That very attitude in life is what we are called to as Christians.

> *Not that I have already attained this . . . but I press on*

Here again is a description of each one of us in our Christian pilgrimage. There are moments of arrival in our experience, moments of the awareness of the presence of God, moments which are for us epiphanies and annunciations. But they pass away again, and we must press on until we are given the next experience of encounter with Our Lord.

> *One thing I do . . . I press on toward the goal . . . Christ Jesus*

If there exists an anthology with a title such as *The Best of Paul of Tarsus*, then this sentence has an honoured place. It is a magnificent piece of simple unadorned honesty. Within it there is that wonderfully healthy statement about forgetting what lies behind and straining forward to what lies ahead. There indeed is a succinct prescription for a healthy Christian life. That attitude is expressed unnumbered times in the Bible. God is a God who calls from beyond us, not from behind us. It is important to say this in an age when many Christians wish to remain merely in the past, as if the past is the natural habitat of Our Lord. The image in the words "the upward call" is so vivid. We are asked to see Our Lord calling and encouraging us in our journey from a point which he occupies, a point both beyond and higher than where we are.

Third Reading *Six days before the Passover, Jesus came to Bethany*

The outwardly simple statement is yet another reminder of his utter humanity. Bethany was home away from home. Bethany meant friends, a place to relax, a place where no role had to be played, no mask had to be worn. We all very badly need our "Bethany" where we know we are accepted and loved, where we don't have to earn that in any way. The image in the words "there they made him a supper" emphasizes the humanity of it all. One wonders what he liked best? Did he eat his vegetables? Did he compliment the cook? That may sound silly but it isn't. It helps to remind us that in spite of stained glass window portraits he is utterly real and human.

Lazarus was one of those at table with him

I note the statement because of its wonderful casualness. There is no regarding of Lazarus as something freakish. Here he is tucking into his supper with the rest of them, presumably passing the salt, asking for seconds, chatting about the current Bethany gossip!

> *Mary took a pound of costly ointment*

The scene that follows remained etched on the memories of those present. In different ways they preserved it in the records of the community. In the light of what was to happen very soon after, they came to see it as a sign of the terrifying future awaiting their Master. Mary's intention remains a mystery. Was it a desperate device to communicate a love she felt and could no longer hide? We will never know that, but the scene is one which calls to our own Christian commitment. How costly to us is what we offer to Our Lord? That is one of the questions Mary's action puts to us across the centuries. Another question she asks us is whether we are ever moved so deeply by our Christian allegiance that we must show what we feel by some action or by some gift.

> *The house was filled with the fragrance of the ointment*

For some reason the statement has a haunting quality. Mary's ointment sends its fragrance not only through that long-ago house in Bethany but through the whole history of all Christian generations. It demands that we bring our own costly gift, whatever that may be, and offer it.

> *Why was this ointment not sold . . . and given to the poor?*

It is not an entirely unreasonable question. In all Christian communities it is occasionally asked about some gesture made, some gift given, some financial decision taken. And it will never entirely be resolved, this tension between pragmatism and symbolism. At the time of writing, the Roman Catholic Church in Poland is about to build a huge new cathedral. Most certainly there are voices who say that the money should be given to those in need in that vast community. On the other hand, the building may become a very potent symbol around which courage and hope and determination may gather in that country. The end result may be far more beneficial to the future of Poland than if the money (always presuming it could be raised) were used for charitable purposes. There is something of this very argument in Our Lord's response to Judas's criticism of Mary's action. The fact of the matter is that human nature needs symbols of mystery and beauty which inspire the motivation which in turn can be turned into generosity towards existing needs.

Psalm

At first sight the psalm is a strange choice for the threshold of the coming season. Should there be images of laughter and shouts of joy when the shadow of the cross looms? Yet the operative words are perhaps "the Lord has done great things," or "those who sowed with tears will reap with songs of joy." These provide hints of the triumph to come. The seed is the image of burial, the sheaf that of resurrection.